LESSONS FROM THE
ART OF JUGGLING

LESSONS FROM

THE ART OF JUGGLING

. .
. .

HOW TO ACHIEVE YOUR FULL POTENTIAL IN BUSINESS, LEARNING, AND LIFE

MICHAEL J. GELB AND TONY BUZAN

AURUM PRESS

This edition first published in Great Britain
1998 by Aurum Press Ltd,
25 Bedford Avenue, London WC1B 3AT

This edition published by
arrangement with Harmony Books,
a division of Crown Publishers Inc.

A catalogue record for this book
is available from the British Library.

ISBN 1 85410 602 3

3 5 7 9 10 8 6 4 2
1998   2000   2002   2001   1999

Printed in Great Britain by
MPG Books, Bodmin

MICHAEL'S DEDICATION

*To my wife and dream-come-true, Nusa, who embodies,
most spectacularly, the spirit of joy, play, growth,
and love that inspired the creation of
the Juggling Metaphor Method.*

TONY'S DEDICATION

*To Vanda North, my magnificent companion, colleague,
and all-around superbaby, whose indefatigable joy
in learning and teaching sustains and inspires me.*

CONTENTS

ACKNOWLEDGMENTS

From Michael: Thanks to my juggling teachers and partners, including Dennis Masella, Stuart Haber, and Lloyd "Tim" Timberlake; Alexander technique teachers and colleagues, especially Walter Carrington, Paul Collins, and Betty Rajna; aikido masters Dr. Clyde Takeguchi, Harvey Konigsberg, Yoshimitsu Yamada, and Mitsugi Saotome; learning guides J. G. Bennett, Dr. Mort Herskowitz, and Dr. Rudolph Bauer; clients who apply the Juggling Metaphor Method in leading their organizations, especially Ed Bassett, Delano Lewis, Jim D'Agostino, Marv Damsma, Dr. Madhu Jayawant, and Dr. Tom Jenkins; office administrator and creative force Charlene Smith, F.S.P.A. And special thanks to my magnificent friend Tony Buzan, for the gift of Mind Maps and the synergy of our vision.

From Tony: Thanks to my Alexander technique teachers, especially Paul Collins, Chris Stevens, and Walter Carrington; to Minoru Kanetsuka for introducing me to the art of aikido; to my office staff, Carol Coaker, Leslie Bias, and Phillida Wilson; to Dr. Andrew Stringer for his remarkable insights into mind and body; and to my mother Jean Buzan for inspiring my appreciation of lifelong learning. Special thanks to my dearest friend Michael Gelb, who invented the method and embodies masterfully the principles described in this book.

From Michael and Tony: Special thanks to our agent, the sagacious and lovely Muriel Nellis, and her staff, Jane Roberts and Karen Gerwin; our editor at Harmony Books, the perspicacious and savvy Peter Guzzardi and his staff, Sarah Hamlin, Penny Simon, John Fontana; F. M. Alexander and Morihei Ueshiba for their gifts to humanity; the International Jugglers Association, the Global Use Your Head Clubs, and the Brain Trust for their continuing support; and special thanks to our illustrator, the master of Visual Synthesis, Nusa Maal Gelb.

Michael Gelb first learned to juggle in 1973 while attending a ten-month residential study program with J. G. Bennett at the International Academy of Continuous Education in England. In 1974 he returned to the United States, supplementing his income by performing as a juggler in Harvard Square. In 1975, Michael moved to London, where he began a three-year training to become a teacher of the Alexander technique of mind and body integration. At the same time, he was completing research for a master's degree with a special focus on learning and teaching the art of relaxed concentration. As part of his research, Gelb decided to attain a high level of proficiency in juggling and to develop a means of using juggling to communicate his ideas on learning how to learn; thus the Juggling Metaphor Method was born. Gelb supported his research by teaching juggling and performing in nightclubs, at festivals, on the street, and at concerts, including appearances with the Rolling Stones and Bob Dylan.

While Gelb was conducting his research, Tony Buzan was busy perfecting his discovery of Mind Mapping, editing the *International Mensa Journal*, writing his bestselling book *Use Both Sides of Your Brain*, and writing and starring in an award-winning program on learning how to learn for BBC television. He also found the time to write a prize-winning book of poetry and conduct his own research into mind/body fitness, which included a personal study of the Alexander technique.

Just as he was beginning to write his master's thesis, Gelb learned Mind Mapping from Buzan. Applying the Mind Mapping method, Gelb wrote his master's thesis, which was eventually published and remains in print in more than fifteen countries. At the same time, Gelb introduced Buzan to the Juggling Metaphor Method. This was the beginning of an extraordinary collaboration and friendship. In 1978, Gelb and Buzan combined their talents to create the Mind and Body Seminar, an extraordinary five-day training for leaders. In 1985, they began making the Mind Maps that would eventually become *Lessons from the Art of Juggling*

Whether teaching together or separately, both Gelb and Buzan use the Juggling Metaphor Method as an integral part of their seminars. Their students include senior executives and other representatives of companies including Amoco, Du Pont, Merck, AT&T, Bell Atlantic, Xerox, and Goldman Sachs; education associations, superintendents, principals, teachers, and students of all ages, including a group of 2,000 children in Soweto, South Africa; the U.S. Army, National Guard, the police academies of northern Virginia and metropolitan London, and many other groups such as the Young Presidents Organization, the Nightingale-Conant Corporation, the British Olympic rowing and chess teams, and National Public Radio.

OPENING POEM

I,
Juggler,
Stand between two spheres.
The expression
Of my Enlightened thoughts
Goes out
And up
To the Sun.
The soles
And balls
Of my feet
Hug the loam of the Earth,
As I weave the dancing patterns of Infinity.

Deeply,
I am a juggler.
Deeply
I breathe out into the Universe
I have breathed
In.

I, Atomic Child,
Charmed Child,
Star Child
Of the Universe,
Juggle
And
Am
Juggled.

INTRODUCTION

Our beliefs and assumptions have a tremendous effect on our perceptions and the results we achieve in life. Many of us hold beliefs that limit our potential and the way we process learning. Formed in the first few years of our lives, these fundamental attitudes often remain unexamined and unconscious.

You have probably picked up this book because you have begun to explore your own learning process and hope to unleash your full power as a learner. Perhaps you are already aware of your ability to change your assumptions and beliefs, and are engaged in a process of choosing those that contribute to the greatest fulfillment and success. Maybe you'd just like to learn how to juggle.

In either case, *Lessons from the Art of Juggling* is for you! It is based on the following propositions that we will explore together:

1. You can learn to juggle . . . and, should you choose to, you *will* learn to juggle . . . and your improvement is inevitable.
2. You will be able to apply the lessons of learning to juggle to learning anything.

3. *Learning how to learn* is life's most important skill.

4. Learning is an intrinsically rewarding and joyful process.

5. Your potential as a learner is virtually unlimited, and your learning ability can improve with age.

6. The greatest learners are distinguished by a mind and body attitude of relaxed concentration. They combine a commitment to excellence with a positive approach to mistakes. If you apply the lessons that follow, you will become one of them!

Research shows that you begin learning in the womb and go right on learning until the moment you pass on. Your brain has a capacity for learning that is virtually limitless, which makes every human a potential genius. By learning how to learn you can access this genius.

TO JUGGLE OR NOT TO JUGGLE . . .

If you purchased this book because you actually want to learn to juggle, then get three balls (tennis balls, lacrosse balls, in a pinch you can use oranges, apples, etc.; no eggs just yet), and practice the juggling exercises as you read. To have more fun and get more feedback, practice with a partner whenever possible. If you already know how to juggle, *Lessons from the Art of Juggling* offers you the opportunity to take a giant step forward in juggling and in all of your life's endeavors.

If you've picked up this book with the idea that you're interested in learning how to learn, but you're not particularly keen on becoming a juggler, we recommend that you *pretend* that you are interested in learning to juggle. Read the instructional chapters, and participate in the exercises.

As you read and practice, the parallels between juggling and various elements of your own personal and professional life will become increasingly clear. As the parallels emerge, you'll become able to apply the Juggling Metaphor Method to whatever discipline you choose.

This book is written in a way that aims to model its message. While the information is communicated in a playful tone and juggling itself is an essentially light-hearted activity (the word *juggler* comes from the Latin root *joculari,* meaning "jest"), the subject of learning how to learn is serious. The approach to learning presented in this book has been field tested with tens of thousands of people from all over the world in our corporate and public seminars. Of course, you will do the most important testing for yourself by applying the suggestions, experiments, and opportunities that follow.

*In a time of drastic change, it is
the learners who inherit the future.
The learned find themselves equipped to live in
a world that no longer exists.*

ERIC HOFFER

PART 1

THE ADVENTURE

BEGINS

1

. .

THE JUGGLING METAPHOR

The greatest thing by far is to be a master of metaphor.

—ARISTOTLE

Consider the simple beauty and elegance of juggling. Observe the accomplished juggler and witness the qualities of balance, poise, rhythm, and playfulness. These are the signs of mastery and excellence toward which everyone openly or secretly strives.

The path to such magnificence is often paved with calamitous experiments, fears of failure, and secret doubts. After well-intentioned—often unsuccessful—attempts, many begin to suspect that this capacity for mind/body mastery and poise can belong only to a handful of naturally gifted people.

We know that feeling! Our own experiences were similar. As a child, Tony regularly caught balls with the wrong parts of his body, ending up with bruised toes, sprained thumbs, and the occasional black eye. In view of these unhappy experiences with spherical objects,

Tony happily agreed with his physical education teachers that he should move to other activities during sports periods.

Michael had easier initial access to his own natural ball sense but never fully developed it until he applied the principles in this book. As children, we never dreamed that one day we would be juggling before audiences as large as 250,000 people. Nor would we have imagined that we would be teaching the art and science of juggling to senior executives of Fortune 500 companies, royalty, army officers, factory workers, schoolteachers, other professionals, students, and children of all ages. Or that we would find ourselves working together on a book that uses playing with balls as a metaphor for all human learning.

WHY JUGGLING AS A LEARNING METAPHOR?

Any learning experience provides a valuable opportunity to revisit fundamental principles of growth and change. Over the past twenty-five years, we have complemented our academic research into the brain and learning with practical tests. We've challenged ourselves continually to learn new things—particularly things for which we'd been told, as children, we had little or no talent. We've learned many new skills such as singing, swimming, ballroom dancing, tennis, languages, martial arts, drawing, and juggling.

Any one of these subjects could provide a fertile metaphor for exploring the art of learning and life. But juggling offers something special. We chose juggling as the focus of our book because learning anything involves keeping a number of things "up in the air" at the same time, because "dropping the balls" provides an ideal metaphor for gracefully coping with mistakes, which we consider to be one of life's most important abilities. Juggling also promotes a sense of inner quiet in the midst of activity, a special experience of mind and body in harmony. And juggling's essential light-heartedness encourages easy access to the fundamental human learning modality of play.

Juggling is easy to learn and offers equal opportunity to both genders and to people of all ages. You can do it on your own or with others, and all you need to begin with is more balls than hands. Progress in juggling is easy to measure, and you can continue improving throughout your life.

Moreover, juggling echoes a universal movement; from the dance of electrons around the nucleus of an atom and the arc of a leaf lifted by wind, to the swirling patterns of galaxies in an ever-expanding universe. Architecture, music, painting, poetry—all seek to express various dimensions of nature's intrinsic pattern. In a simple, immediate way, the art of juggling aligns us with this essential universal rhythm, echoing a pattern that links us with all creation and resonates with our deepest selves.

As George Leonard writes in *The Silent Pulse*, "At the heart of each of us, whatever our imperfections, there exists a silent pulse of perfect rhythm, a complex of wave forms and resonances, which is absolutely individual and unique, and yet which connects us to everything in the universe. The act of getting in touch with this pulse can transform our personal experience and in some way alter the world around us."

Learning to juggle will help you discover your own perfect rhythm. You will find that learning to sense and trust this "silent pulse" is the key to fulfillment in learning and life. After more than sixty combined years of studying high performance in individuals and organizations, we've developed an approach to learning that accelerates progress and maximizes enjoyment. We begin by taking you through a step-by-step approach to learning to juggle. In the succeeding chapters you will learn how to:

- Set goals and visualize results based on evolving models of excellence.
- Transform your attitude toward mistakes and failure.
- Recognize and change limiting habitual patterns in yourself.
- Reattain your natural poise by cultivating the art of relaxed concentration.
- Develop your coaching skills so you can initiate others into the joyful journey of lifelong learning.
- Unleash your natural genius through the power of play!

AFTER LESSONS FROM THE ART . . .

When you have completed the exercises in this book, you will begin to enjoy many other specific and lifelong benefits, including:

1. balance and ambidexterity
2. fitness
3. relaxed concentration/appropriate effort
4. enjoyment and confidence

Let's take these vitally important subjects one at a time.

BALANCE AND AMBIDEXTERITY

Juggling develops ambidexterity. It promotes rhythmic coordination between the two sides of the body and the two sides of the brain. Ambidexterity offers an important key to high performance and balanced living.

Although we have studied ambidexterity for many years, its true importance was highlighted for us when we met Professor Raymond Dart, the renowned brain researcher, anthropologist, and anatomist. Professor Dart also overcame, in his eighties, an apparently irreversible progressive blindness. He explained to us in detail how he did so. He began by conducting an exhaustive analysis of his movement patterns, which revealed a tendency to become progressively physically unbalanced—as he put it, "filled with millions of creaks." He trained himself to use his body in a more balanced way, most especially to develop the balanced use of both hands and both sides of the body. He reported significant improvements in both his eyesight and general functioning as a result of his experiment with ambidexterity.

At the end of our glorious day with him, we asked Professor Dart to sum up his life's work with five major messages he would give to the children of the future. He replied that there was only one message and, rising from his chair, exclaimed, "Michael, Tony, you must go out and tell people to balance their brains, balance their bodies. The future lies with the ambidextrous human!" Professor Dart's message is supported by recent research showing that a balanced brain tends to produce a more balanced body, and that a balanced body similarly encourages a more balanced brain.

Professor Dart recommended juggling as a training

device to attain this naturally poised human state. He confirmed to us that his observations of superior performance in a variety of human activities showed an unexpectedly high percentage of ambidextrous individuals. In sports, for example, many of the "all time great" athletes were and are ambidextrous. Examples include boxing champions Jack Dempsey, Joe Louis, Sugar Ray Robinson, Muhammad Ali, and Julio César Chavez. Baseball stars such as Mickey Mantle and Willie Mays, and basketball greats such as Larry Bird, Magic Johnson, and Michael Jordan are all ambidextrous.

In the arts, two artists many regard as the most accomplished of all time, Leonardo da Vinci and Michelangelo, consciously cultivated their ambidexterity. Michelangelo, for example, regularly amazed his students and other observers by switching hands while sculpting his masterpieces. Recent studies by Dr. Frederick Leboyer of children born in the most supportive environments have shown that a significant percentage of these children naturally developed a high degree of ambidextrous behavior.

Juggling fosters rhythmic coordination between the two sides of the body and the two sides of the brain. Regular juggling builds psychophysical ambidexterity.

FITNESS

In addition to ambidexterity, juggling offers a number of other fitness-related benefits: lively muscle tone, quickened reflexes, refined hand-eye coordination, and subtle balance and poise. And in the early stages, picking up your juggling balls can provide considerable aerobic training! As you progress you can build upper-body strength and power by juggling heavy objects. Juggling can also be combined with running ("joggling") and dancing ("jiggling") to provide aerobic benefit to the advanced student.

RELAXED CONCENTRATION/APPROPRIATE EFFORT

By learning to learn and juggle through applying the principles in *Lessons from the Art of Juggling,* you will discover how to divide your attention appropriately between different pressing elements, while simultaneously maintaining an awareness of the "whole picture." When learning to juggle, you must both relax and focus at the same time. This quality of *relaxed concentration* is essential to high performance in any discipline.

When you watch a great performer like Fred Astaire, Ella Fitzgerald, Joe Montana, or Meryl Streep, you notice that they make it look easy. As you learn to juggle, you will soon discover that the best results are achieved by using the right amount of effort in the right place at the right time. And this right amount is usually less than we think we need.

In other words, the less unnecessary effort you put into learning, the more successful you will be. In this approach to learning and juggling you will learn to let go of unnecessary tension, shedding inappropriate neck, shoulder, torso, and other body movements. You will discover that the secret of juggling—the key to faster learning—is to use *appropriate effort.*

Most of us are used to getting results by trying harder, but with some things trying harder does not work. As Yoda says in *Star Wars,* "Try? There is no try. There is only do or not do."

Greater effort can exacerbate faulty patterns of action. Doing the wrong thing with more intensity rarely improves the situation. Learning something new often requires us to unlearn something old. As you learn to learn and learn to juggle we'll show you how to undo old patterns of tension and stress, how to get more result with less effort. In the process you will discover the beauty of "stillness in activity." This state of harmony, flow, or grace will positively influence every area of your life.

ENJOYMENT AND CONFIDENCE

Perhaps for the first time since your early childhood, when like all children you naturally loved learning, you will find that learning new things—even things for which you think you have little talent—can be engaging, enjoyable, and fun. You'll discover that the process of learning offers its own intrinsic rewards. As you learn to juggle you will discover that it is a highly enjoyable activity. The movement, colors, sensations, and rhythms provide a never-ending source of amusement and joy.

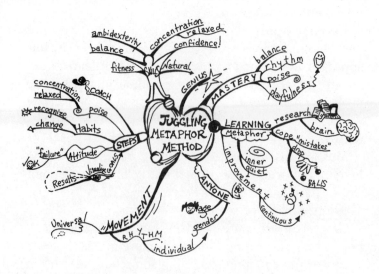

And, as you progress you'll experience an artist's delight in creating moving sculptures.

We will show you how to juggle and how to learn by building on a series of small successes. Each time you succeed your confidence will grow, inspiring you onward to greater success. Confidence builds success and success builds confidence. The lessons that follow will show you how to create this "virtuous cycle."

As you develop an understanding of your phenomenal learning power, and a command of the strategies for accessing it, your confidence will blossom. Applying the lessons that follow, you will learn to do things you may have previously thought impossible.

2

MASTERING INFINITY

*To see a world in a grain of sand
and heaven in a wild flower,
hold infinity in the palm of your hand
and eternity in an hour.*

—WILLIAM BLAKE
"Auguries of Innocence"

THE ART OF JUGGLING

On our journey of learning to learn and learning to juggle we take you back to 1974, when Michael was first inspired to juggle. He saw a brilliant juggler throwing three balls in a sideways figure-eight pattern. Michael exclaimed, "The infinity symbol! He's holding infinity in his hands!" Amazed and inspired, Michael decided at that moment to master the infinity pattern and to become a juggler himself. He asked the performing genius in question to teach him. The juggler agreed, but his teaching skill did not match his juggling ability. The only instruction he gave was: "Take these three balls, throw them up, and don't let any of them drop!"

The instructions you receive in this book will be more helpful, more detailed, and will guarantee your success in every step of the learning process. Let's begin by setting the stage for a successful juggling experience.

YOUR EXTERNAL LEARNING ENVIRONMENT

The quality of your environment has a powerful influence on the learning process. Whether you are studying for an exam, learning to play the piano, or attending a seminar you'll learn faster and more effectively with appropriate space, natural lighting, fresh air, the right equipment, and in some cases, the right music. Let's consider now the ideal environment for learning to juggle.

1. SPACE: You can, and eventually will, juggle everywhere! In the early stages of your juggling, however, you will want to create a supportive environment. If you are juggling indoors, select an area with high ceilings, plenty of room, and a minimum number of breakable objects. Hills, valleys, fields, yards, and beaches are ideal places to juggle because natural beauty echoes the patterns of juggling, and the ceilings are sky-high.

2. LIGHT: The ideal light for juggling is natural sunlight. When this is not available, full-spectrum or incandescent lights are the best substitutes. Avoid practicing your juggling under fluorescent light, as it creates eye stress and interferes with the integration of your left and right brain hemispheres. Poor lighting can also disrupt your physical balance and disturb your perception of form and shape.

3. AIR: Weighing in at only two to three percent of your body's weight, your brain uses 20 percent of your body's oxygen. Therefore, it is important, whenever possible, to juggle in a space where there is good ventilation and fresh air.

4. MUSIC: The right music will awaken your sense of rhythm and will help balance your brain. We recommend that you provide yourself with music while practicing in order to derive these benefits. Musical selections we enjoy while juggling include those composed or performed by: Vivaldi, Bach, Mozart, Beethoven, Glenn Miller, Andreas Vollenweider, R. Carlos Nakei, Jean-Michel Jarre, and Tina Turner.

If musical equipment is unavailable, you can make up your own tunes, songs, and rhythms. Hum. Whistle. Sing to yourself. Tap out rhythms. Create your own juggling music!

5. EQUIPMENT: As you become more proficient at juggling, you will find that any objects that are not tied down and that you can lift are jugglable. However, to begin with, we recommend:

   a. Balls: Initially you will need three balls. Professional jugglers often use lacrosse balls, although tennis balls, racquet balls—indeed any balls that you can throw and catch easily and comfortably, and that appeal to your senses—will be appropriate. We recommend that the three balls be of different colors and especially that at least *one* be a different color. This will help make it easier for you to discriminate between juggling patterns, and will make it easier to learn new and advanced techniques.

b. *Scarves:* To boost your confidence, you may wish to experiment by juggling light, one-square-foot silk scarves. Scarves have the advantage of floating in the air when tossed, creating a *slow motion* juggling experience.

c. *Bean Bags:* Note: While bean bags are popular juggling objects and have the apparent advantage of not bouncing when dropped, they are fundamentally static and may limit your possibilities for creative juggling. Balls create a livelier feeling in your hands. And, in addition to creating a pleasant sound, the bouncing ball offers valuable feedback on the appropriateness of the strength and direction of your throw. Moreover, the bounce of a fallen ball can itself become the impetus for new juggling tricks.

6. BALL MANAGEMENT: When Michael was first learning to juggle, he regularly dropped the balls on the floor. Shortly thereafter, he was informed by his landlord that if he continued to play drums on his neighbor's ceiling, he would be evicted. So Michael developed solutions such as "The Bed" and "The Couch," described below.

a. *The Bed:* Juggle, standing beside a bed, so when the balls fall, they land on the bed, not on the floor!

b. *The Couch or Hammock:* Similar to the bed, a couch or hammock can help you manage your balls.

c. *The Parachute:* For the total enthusiast, a parachute or large sheet can be attached to the four corners of a room, forming a bowl in which the juggler stands at the center. The advantage of this is that all of the balls will roll back to you whenever they drop.

7. As You Progress: You may decide you'd like to perform publicly as a juggler. In that case, we suggest preparing yourself by occasionally practicing in conditions exactly *opposite* to those described above! Most performance venues such as nightclubs, the street, parties, and so on, have low ceilings, fetid air, glaring lights, and other distractions. Start with the best conditions and "work your way down."

YOUR INTERNAL LEARNING ENVIRONMENT

WARM-UP: Before you start to juggle, warm up. Practice your favorite stretches, yoga postures, aikido, or tai chi exercises, or make up your own routine.

MAINTAIN AN UPRIGHT POSTURE: The best juggling posture is upright but not rigid, like a Masai warrior or a healthy baby. Place your feet shoulder-width apart. Stand at your full height. Let your shoulders rest easily on your torso, with your entire body in alignment and your head freely balanced on top. Keep your elbows close to the sides of your body. Your joints are flexible and springy rather than locked.

BREATHE FREELY: Throughout your juggling, monitor yourself and check that you are still breathing! Many people, especially in the early stages, will hold their breath when throwing and catching the balls. Allow yourself to breathe fully and freely, occasionally allowing a deep and extended exhalation (sighing and yawning are useful). Every now and then, test the ease and freedom of your breathing by making an extended whispered *ahhhh* sound.

COMMIT YOURSELF TO LEARNING: If you commit yourself to learning and practice juggling according to the following instructions, you will inevitably make progress. You will, however, experience the ups and downs that are a natural part of learning any new skill. The adjacent graph illustrates the inevitable and neces-

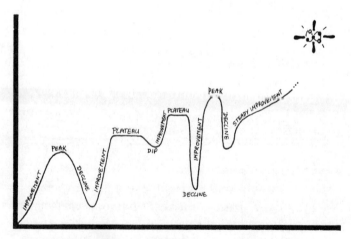

ELEMENTS OF IMPROVEMENT AND PROGRESS

sary stages of the learning process as it relates to your juggling and all your learning activities. These stages include:

- *Plateaus*—during which you will appear to be making little progress but will, on a subconscious level, be integrating for the next leap forward
- *Steep or small declines*—when you drop old habits but haven't quite developed new ones, it often seems as if you are getting worse despite your practice. These periods of decline frequently precede major leaps forward.
- Periods of *sharp improvement or steady progress*—when your brain/body system successfully integrates the fruits of your practice

Of course, your own graph will be different from any other individual's graph, but it will contain all of the same elements. At the outset of learning juggling or any other skill, it is important to know that these stages *must* appear in your graph; that when you experience any apparent setbacks, they are a natural part of the learning process, and that they are, in fact, major guides that can *help* your progress. As you become familiar with the natural progression of your learning graph, you'll be able to relax and enjoy every part of it. And, as you learn to relax you'll learn faster

---

Conscious Dropping; Attention to Process—*One of the secrets of our approach to learning to juggle is to drop the balls on purpose. In our juggling classes we demonstrate the three-ball cascade and ask our students to observe carefully. We ask them to describe what they notice about the movement of our hands. After noting that our hands are moving* *in a simple, rhythmic, up and down, outward circular pattern, someone usually points out that our hands are moving in a totally consistent manner. We then ask the class "What makes it possible to move your hands in the same way every time?" Someone usually answers, "Practice!" Of course, this is true, but the real secret is* practicing throwing the balls to the same place every time *so that they will land in the same place consistently. This makes juggling easy! It is therefore essential in the early stages to focus primarily on the throw and not the catch. This is accomplished by consciously dropping the balls.*

ONE-BALL JUGGLING INSTANT SUCCESS!

START BY PLAYING WITH ONE BALL: Take one ball and play with it, experimenting as creatively as you can. Try all kinds of throwing, positions for catching, and variations on whatever themes you imagine. Throw the ball high; bounce it off the ground; enjoy the feeling of letting the ball drop. Many of the great jugglers create the basic elements of their new routines by going back to one-ball experimentation and play.

VISUALIZE THE JUGGLER'S BOX: The juggler's box can be used as the fundamental framework for all your juggling. Imagine a box of space, the bottom plane of which is located at the level of your navel; the top plane is located approximately six inches above the top of your head. Your hands rest on the bottom plane of the box, relaxed and open; forearms are roughly parallel with the ground and elbows are close to your body.

Balls thrown from your right hand are aimed at the point to the left of center of the top of the box. When you hit this point the ball will land in your left hand. Balls thrown from your left hand are aimed at the point to the right of center of the top of the box. When you hit this point the ball will land in your right hand.

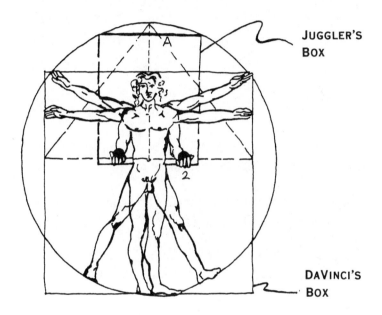

JUGGLER'S
BOX

DaVINCI'S
BOX

JUGGLE ONE BALL: Your first juggling exercise is to throw a ball to the top of the box at the point marked "A," letting the ball land in your other hand at the position marked "2."

When throwing the ball, release it with minimal effort: simply flex the elbow and wrist slightly, sending the ball off your fingertips to the point at the top of the box. An artist described the first step by saying, "The effect is like that of a small wave starting with a

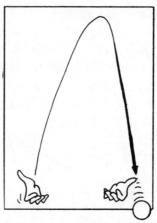

THROWING AND LETTING ONE BALL DROP!

gleam in the eye, pulsing through the elbow, ending
with the hand's final splash, cascading the ball into the
air."

Your first throw will be received by your other hand,
which is waiting in its original position at the bottom
plane of the "box." You needn't grasp the ball, just receive it openly and easily. If your throw doesn't land
near your waiting hand, do not lunge for it, *let it drop*.
Then pause. Take a deep breath, and reinforce your
mental image of where you want your throw to go.

Monitor your posture, balance, and breathing, focusing on releasing the ball consistently with minimal effort. As you incorporate the mechanics of one-ball
juggling, you will begin to discover a pleasing rhythm.

Focus your eyes softly. *People often ask: "Where should I
look? Where should my eyes be focused while I'm juggling?"
Softly focus your eyes at the apex of the ball's flight, i.e., the
appropriate point at the top of the box. This allows your
peripheral vision to take in all the information you'll need to*

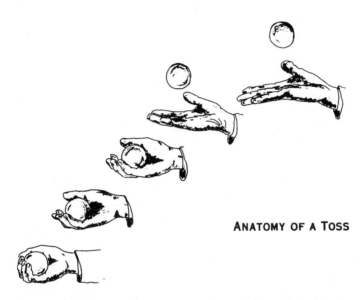

ANATOMY OF A TOSS

juggle accurately. Keep your eyes softly focused and your hands will automatically adjust to the appropriate receiving position. There is no need to look at your hands as your kinaesthetic sense provides a reliable guide to their location.

Let catching take care of itself. *Have you ever had some-one toss something your way and discovered quite unexpect-edly that you caught it without thinking? This catching reflex is a natural ability that emerges when we are not worried about "trying to catch." In the early stages of your juggling, keep your attention on the quality of your throws and let catching take care of itself.*

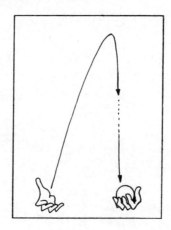

THROWING AND CATCHING ONE BALL

TWO BALLS

Congratulations! You now know everything you need to know to be a masterful one-ball juggler. But to really impress your friends you will probably want to learn more. The good news is that juggling two or three balls requires doing exactly what you have done with one, sequentially. The simple steps are:

STEP ONE: *Throwing and Dropping Two Balls.* Place one ball in each hand, calling the first ball to be thrown "1" and the second "2." In our illustrations 1 (your first throw) is light, and 2 is dark.

Throw ball 1 to the appropriate point at the top of the box exactly the same way you did in the previous exercise (one-ball juggling). As your first throw reaches its apex, throw ball 2 to its corresponding destination at the top of the box. Let both balls drop. *Don't even think about attempting to catch them.* Success at this

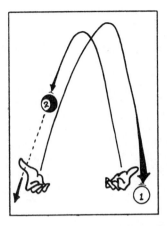

THROWING AND DROPPING TWO BALLS

stage is defined as being able to throw the balls to the top of the box in staggered timing and *letting them drop* with élan.

If the balls have been thrown to their respective points at the top of the box, they will land, in staggered timing, a few inches in front of your feet. We are counting on you to be 100 percent successful in letting the balls *drop*.

STEP TWO: *Allowing One Ball to Be Caught.* Success in step two is based upon giving yourself the following brain-compatible instructions: "I am going to take these two balls and throw them up to the top of the box in staggered timing (as in step one), and if the first one happens to land in the immediate vicinity of my hand, I will allow it to be caught." Practice this step until the first ball begins to land in your hand. Remember to let the second ball drop.

STEP THREE: *Allowing Both Balls to Be Caught.* This step is identical to step two, the only addition being

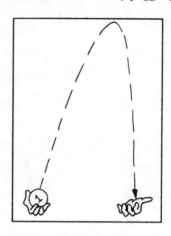

ONE BALL

that you allow *both* balls to land in your hands. Should they not be falling in the general area of your hands, let them drop! Be careful not to *hand* the second ball across the bottom plane of the box. Throw each ball, in staggered timing, to its respective point at the top of the box. Concentrate throughout on the accuracy of your *throw*, allowing the catching to take care of itself.

TWO BALLS

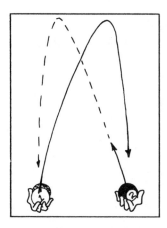

READY FOR THREE BALLS

After you have practiced with two balls for ten to twenty minutes, move on to the first stages of three-ball juggling—even if you have not mastered the two-ball stage. Many of our students protest: "How can I possibly do three when I have not mastered two?" We find that *by stretching yourself beyond your perceived level of competence you accelerate your development of competence.* This general learning principle is perfectly reflected in making the leap from two to three balls. After attempting three balls and stretching yourself beyond your apparent limits, two balls will seem easier. And many people discover that the natural rhythm of three-ball juggling becomes easier than two-ball juggling.

THREE-BALL JUGGLING: YOUR FIRST JUGGULATION!

STEP ONE: *Throwing and Dropping Three Balls.* Take two balls in one hand, one ball in the other hand. The

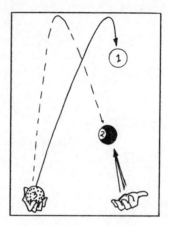

THREE-BALL JUGGLING

hand with two balls will always be the one with which you start. (As you progress with your practicing try alternating your starting hand, beginning first with two balls in one hand and then starting with two balls in the other to further facilitate your ambidexterity.) Call the front ball in the hand with two balls 1, the single ball in your other hand is 2, and the rear ball (the one closer to your wrist) in the hand with two balls will be the third throw; hence, we call it ball number 3!

Throw ball 1 to its point at the top of the box. As it reaches the apex, throw the second ball to its point at the top of the box. As ball 2 reaches its apex, throw the *third* ball, to its point at the top of the box (the same place you aimed your first throw). Let each ball drop, as in the previous exercise.

Practice releasing the balls in a fluid rhythm without even thinking of catching. Focus on where you want the balls to go (the points at the top of the box) and enjoy letting them drop. Continue experimenting with your rhythm until you are dropping all three balls with panache!

STEP TWO: *Throwing Three, Allowing One to Be Caught.* Throw the three balls up as in step one. This time, allow the first ball to land in your opposite hand. Let the other two drop.

STEP THREE: *Throwing Three Balls, Allowing Two to Be Caught.* Throw the three balls as in step two, and this time, allow the *first and second* (1 and 2) balls to land in your hands, while letting ball 3 drop. You will notice that when the two balls land in your hands, there is only one ball left in the air . . . and you can already juggle one ball. It really is easier than you thought, isn't it?

STEP FOUR: *Your First Juggulation: Throwing Three Balls, Letting Three Be Caught.* Throw the three balls as in the previous steps, allowing all three balls to be caught if they are in the vicinity of your hands. When you have accomplished this—the tossing and catching

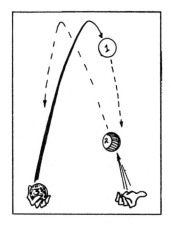

CASCADING START

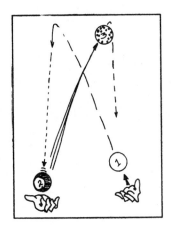

CASCADING

of all three balls—you will have achieved your first juggulation. Celebrate.

MULTIPLE JUGGULATIONS!

To continue past your first juggulation, you simply keep
on throwing the balls! Focus your attention on continuing to *throw*, without worrying about catching.

Your fourth throw will be the same ball that you
started with (1), but this time, you will be throwing it
with the opposite hand because that is where it will
have landed after you threw it the first time. (Remember to make this first/fourth ball a different color, so
that you can immediately recognize it as the ball that
you have to throw.)

At this stage, it is useful to go back to the image of
the box, checking the height, trajectory, and timing of
your throws. Be sure that your shoulders haven't crept
up to your ears, and that you're breathing freely.

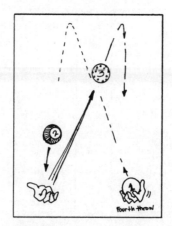

FOURTH THROW IS FIRST BALL

Now simply instruct yourself to "throw, throw, throw, throw, . . . " directing the balls to the points at the top of the box. Let the catching take care of itself and enjoy dropping the balls when you do. Seek a fluid, easy rhythm. If you find yourself getting stuck or frustrated, pause; breathe fully; carry on. If you're still stuck, return for a minute or two to an earlier stage of the process (i.e., letting three balls drop; two balls drop; one-ball juggling; and so on).

As you practice, experiment; listen to music, sing, pretend you are the world's greatest juggler. Have fun. The most important thing to remember is to focus on the quality of your throws and your own poise. As your throwing improves, the balls will increasingly land in your hands, effortlessly.

JUGGLING TOWARD INFINITY

When we are asked how we learned to juggle, we sometimes tell the story of the time we were walking down a street and saw three balls moving in an infinity pattern in space. We stood behind them and have been there ever since! We call this infinitely graceful state, where juggling seems to happen by itself, the "juggling flow state."

You will notice that your three-ball pattern approximates a figure eight lying on its side, the common symbol for infinity. We recommend that you set as your ultimate goal the ability to juggle infinitely, to access the juggling flow state.

Once you have completed your first juggulation, you may wish to set yourself a progressive series of goals toward infinity. We recommend the following:

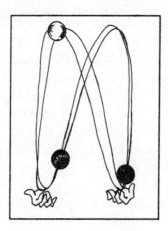

INFINITY PATTERN IN SPACE

- 4 accurate throws
- 5 accurate throws
- 6 accurate throws, 2 continuous juggulations (When you attain 6 throws—2 three-ball circuits— you will have exceeded the boundary of static juggulations, entering the realm of the juggling flow state.)
- 9 throws (3 complete continuous juggulations)
- 21 throws (7 complete continuous juggulations)
- 100 throws (33.3 complete continuous juggulations)
- 1,000 throws (333.3 complete continuous juggulations)

At this point, the thrill of counting the number of your accurate throws may begin to wane. Instead, you can set time-measured goals for maintaining the juggling flow state (i.e., 30 seconds, a minute, five minutes, and then whatever personal marathon goals you choose).

You can take your "juggling pulse" by timing yourself for a minute, counting the number of complete continuous juggulations (CCJs). In this way, you can keep an idea of how many CCJs you are completing in the time you maintain the juggling flow state. As we go to press, the world record in linear time is 2 hours and 58 minutes. If you are going to go for it, give priority to the quality and ease of your process.

For those who desire a more formal grading system we have included the Milestones to Infinity: The Master Juggler Grid in the Appendix that will help you measure your progress toward your jugglerian black belt.

DETOURS ON THE PATH: THE CLASSICAL CHALLENGES

In every stage of learning to juggle, you will encounter interesting challenges to your ability to maintain the juggling flow state. Here are some of the classical experiences:

1. *COLLIDING BALLS*

Challenge: The balls bang into one another.

Solution: Although in your advanced juggling you may wish to bounce the balls together in space as a trick, you'll need to make an adjustment if it is happening unintentionally.

Colliding balls are usually caused either by an overly narrow trajectory (i.e., throwing the balls straight up) or by throwing a ball before the previous throw has reached its apex (i.e., throwing the second ball too soon).

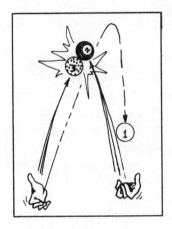

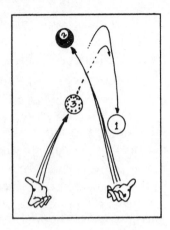

COLLIDING BALLS

**SOLUTION: FOCUS ON
THE THROW**

To ensure the appropriate trajectory, check your throws to (1) make sure that the first ball is thrown to the appropriate point at the top of the box, and (2) that the second ball is thrown to its appropriate point at the top of the box, in such a way as to go *underneath the flight path of the first ball.*

To prevent premature throwing, wait until the first throw has reached its apex *before* releasing the next ball.

2. *SHOWERING INSTEAD OF CASCADING*

Challenge: Showering is the direct passing of the balls from one hand to the other along the lower plane of the box.

The shower is a standard juggling pattern. It tends, however, to exacerbate body asymmetry and to limit the freedom and flexibility in your juggling, and is thus inappropriate until you have mastered the three-ball cascade.

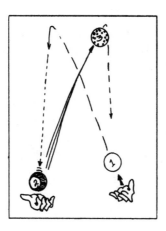

CASCADING

Solution: Throw the first ball to the top of the box and let it drop. Pause for a moment. Visualize where you want the second throw to go. When you're confident that you can throw the second ball to its appropriate apex, do so. When you succeed in throwing the balls accurately, with this pause, decrease the time between throws until the challenge is overcome.

3. ASYMMETRICAL THROWING

Challenge: One hand seems to have a mind of its own (usually your nondominant hand) and is consistently throwing the balls out of the box and out of range of your other hand.

Solution: Observe the energy and direction of the misthrow. Refine your focus on the basic dimensions of the box and where you want the balls to go in space.

If the challenge persists, go back to one-ball practice for a few minutes, focusing on the symmetry of

NO SHOWERING INSTEAD OF CASCADING

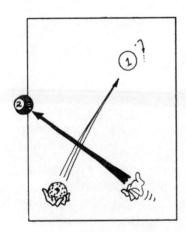

ASYMMETRICAL THROWING

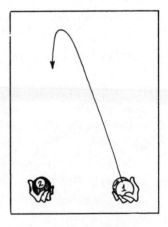

SOLUTION: START WITH OTHER HAND

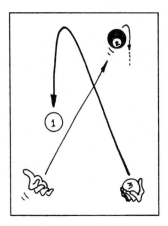

JUGGLING STARTING WITH OTHER HAND

your tosses. This will eventually transfer to your three-ball juggling.

You can also often correct asymmetrical throwing by starting your juggling with your nondominant hand and bringing extra attention to the quality of the throws from that hand.

4. *GETTING STUCK AT THE END OF THE FIRST JUG-GULATION*

Challenge: You've completed your first juggulation, and you don't know how to continue.

Solution: Having achieved your first juggulation, celebrate and be prepared to move on. The secret is to keep the emphasis on throwing. In order to progress, you must be willing to start dropping the balls again, raising yourself to a higher level of chaos.

As you juggle, count aloud with each toss—one, two, three. During your second juggulation, instead of shouting "four, five, six" shout out "throw, throw, throw," tossing a ball with every shout. Keep your attention on throwing, and enjoy the process of throwing and dropping or catching the balls.

5. PROGRESSIVE ACCELERATION

Challenge: This challenge is often rooted in a misconception—that juggling is a speedy, complex activity. This creates a tendency to try *too* hard, rushing after success to avoid perceived failure and losing touch with the natural rhythm of the process. This leads to a self-fulfilling prophecy, which robs your sense of time and space. Physically, this attitude manifests in a decrease in the height of your throws and a raising of your hands to catch the balls at higher and higher levels within the box.

Solution: Refocus your attention on throwing the balls to the *top* of the box while maintaining your hand level nearer the *bottom* plane of the box. To access the appropriate sense of timing and dimension, you may also find it useful to imagine that you are juggling underwater or on the moon. Allow deep

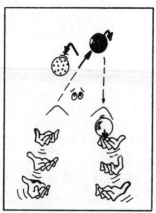
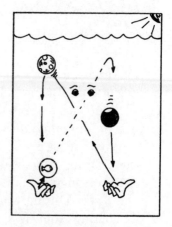

PROGRESSIVE ACCELERATION   SOLUTION: UNDER WATER

exhalations, exaggerate the height of your throws, and let the balls come to you. Remember, if you focus on the throw and your own poise, the balls will land in the same place consistently and you will have plenty of space and time available.

6. *BEING LED AROUND BY THE BALLS*

Challenge: You have a fanatical desire to catch every ball thrown, which is characterized by excessive reaching, grabbing, and lunging, with accompanying body tension and general distress. This challenge is caused by the need to grasp prematurely for results (catching) rather than attending to the process (throwing, breathing).

Solution: Stay exactly where you are and allow the balls to drop if they don't land effortlessly in your hands. It is important that you juggle them rather than let the balls juggle *you!* Juggling while facing a wall will prevent you from lunging forward. You can also walk backward while practicing, thereby shifting

BEING LED AROUND BY THE BALLS

STANDING IN FRONT OF WALL

out of your habit of reaching forward. The essential solution, however, is to maintain your primary focus on the quality and direction of your throws within the box in harmony with the balance of your mind and body.

By now you will see that many of these challenges represent plateaus and downward movements in your individual graph of progress. Rest assured that these are part of the learning process and that if you persevere with the principles of *Lessons from the Art of Juggling* you will inevitably succeed.

GUIDE TO APPLICATION

1. As we mentioned in the beginning of this chapter, Michael's first juggling teacher told him to take three balls, throw them up, and "don't let any of them drop." By making the task so complex Michael's teacher virtually guaranteed that the learning process would begin with a series of

discouraging failures. Instead, we recommend beginning any learning activity with a series of inspiring successes! Approach a new learning challenge by breaking it down into simple, easy-to-manage steps. This approach allows you to build on a series of small successes. Each small success builds greater confidence, and growing confidence supports further success.

2. If you are not making mistakes, then you are not really learning. To learn how to juggle, you have got to be willing to drop the balls. Anticipate unavoidable mistakes such as dropping the balls, and reframe them as integral parts of the learning process. Viewing mistakes as essential parts of the learning process makes any learning faster and more fun.

3. You can accelerate your progress in juggling or any other learning task by beginning with an intensive practice session. Learning can be compared with the flight of a rocket: the greatest energy is required during takeoff. If you want to learn a language, for example, you will find that if you begin with a few days of total immersion, all your subsequent efforts will yield greater results.

4. Once you've launched your new endeavor, experiment with the times of day in which you learn best. Some people learn best first thing in the morning, while others do better just before bedtime. Experiment with your learning biorhythms, and design a consistent practice schedule accordingly.

5. Whether just before a break or at the end of a practice session, finish at a high point. We've never met a basketball player who will leave the

court without making his last shot. Hoopsters seem to understand instinctively the importance of a positive "recency effect." The recency effect is a phenomenon discovered by psychological researchers. It states that you are likely to remember things that happen at the end of a learning session. When you finish on a high note, your strongest memory, until your next practice session, will be of success. This will help you build the confidence that nurtures a positive learning cycle.

6. Cultivate objectivity: watch your juggling or anything else you're attempting to learn as if you were an outside observer. Imagine you are a scientist from another planet, who has come to study the human learning process and that *you* are the subject of the observation!

7. Make short breaks part of your juggling practice.

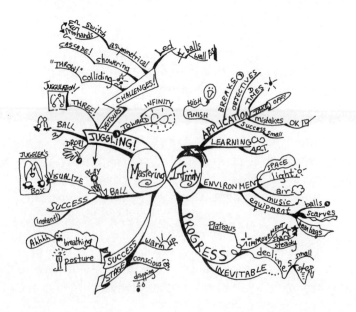

These breaks allow you to integrate, mentally and physically, your most recent learning experience.

Make short juggling breaks a part of your workday. A good regimen is sixty minutes of work followed by five to ten minutes of juggling. In addition to improving your juggling, these breaks will also help you to discover relaxed concentration in your work.

In our juggling classes, we always begin with a demonstration, our attempt to model excellence for the students. In the next chapter we'll explore the importance of models of excellence and an approach that can help *you* become such a model.

PART 2

TOWARD PERFECT PRACTICE

· ·

3

.
.   .

MASTERY BY OSMOSIS

*The quality of a person's life is in direct proportion to
their commitment to excellence,
regardless of their chosen field of endeavor.*

—VINCE LOMBARDI

In the early days of his juggling career, Michael practiced for some time without particularly noticeable
gains. One day while walking in the park, he happened
upon a group of professional jugglers and spent hours
observing while they performed. The following day, as
if by magic, he found he was able to perform many of
the tricks he had witnessed that he had previously been
unable to do—it was as though he had absorbed the
tricks by osmosis. Back then, he did not fully understand the phenomenon, but now we both do. This chapter will show you how to make this learning by osmosis
a conscious process.

MODELS OF EXCELLENCE

1. *JUGGLING IN THE MIND'S EYE*. Any learning process or new activity you decide to pursue—be it juggling, business, sport, academics, or other area of endeavor—begins with the formation of an initial mental image or goal. If you want to learn skiing, you begin with a vague picture in your mind of yourself plummeting down a snowy slope. If you want to learn to scuba dive, you imagine yourself under water. If you're planning to get married, you picture yourself and your partner living happily ever after.

You probably picked up this book because you want to learn how to learn and learn how to juggle. If you've never juggled before, the chances are, in your mind's eye, you start with a vague picture of juggling, perhaps imagining balls or other objects dancing from your hands. If you practiced the exercises in the previous chapter, your mental image of juggling will be clearer and more complete. As you continue to practice and receive instruction, your internal picture of juggling will evolve.

As your mental image evolves, it will expand to include the senses of touch, sound, and kinaesthetic moving awareness. To accelerate your learning, establish multidimensional, multisensory images of excellence at the beginning of all your learning endeavors and now, at the launching of your juggling career.

Baby ducks learn to survive by imitating their mothers. Learning through imitation is fundamental to many species, including humans. As we become adults, we have a unique advantage: we can choose who and what to imitate. We can also consciously choose new models to replace previously imitated but no longer functional models.

Since the learning process begins with the formation of a mental image, you may as well choose the best. If you want to become a great juggler, spend as much time as you can watching great jugglers. If you want to become a great tennis player, observe the best players. If you want to become a leader, study the great leaders.

Whatever your discipline, become a student of excellence in all things. Take every opportunity to observe people who manifest the qualities of mastery. These models of excellence will inspire and guide you toward the fulfillment of your highest potential.

Common sense tells us that in order to achieve success, we must set goals—we must create a vision. Base your goals and nurture your visions with evolving multisensory images of excellence.

2. *THE QUALITIES OF EXCELLENCE*. How can you recognize excellence when you see it? How can you separate the great from the very good? When developing models of excellence in any discipline, seek the following qualities:

Appropriate Effort/Poise. Appropriate effort can be observed in the movements of a cat, a master at a craft, and in the performance of many champions. It involves applying the right amount of energy in the right place at the right time. In other words, the absence of wasted energy, an economy of movement.

Witness the apparently effortless grace of Rubinstein at the piano, Fred Astaire gliding across the dance floor, Muhammad Ali (in his prime) floating like a butterfly (at 225 pounds!), Pete Sampras winning Wimbledon, and Florence Griffith Joyner (Flo Jo) beaming her way to new world records.

Flo Jo's smile, while winning the Olympic gold medal and breaking the world record at the same time, was a perfect example of mind and body in glorious harmony. "She makes it look so easy!" cries the commentator. Such performances are perfect examples of appropriate effort, the natural expression of the human body and mind used according to design.

Commitment to Continuous Learning. On his deathbed, Pierre-Auguste Renoir painted a picture of a flower. As he died, he mused, "I think I'm beginning to understand something about [art]." Renoir possessed the characteristic of all true masters: a lifelong commitment to learning.

Whether they are practicing or involved in competition or creation, masters of all disciplines learn from every aspect of their participation, gathering information equally from their successes, plateaus, and failures. This commitment to continuous improvement is the key to individual excellence. It is also the cornerstone of organizational high performance and is at the heart of the quality movement.

High Standards and Personal Accountability. According to an ancient Japanese proverb, "When you have completed 95 percent of your journey you are only halfway there." The willingness to travel the last 5 percent separates the great from the very good. As Somerset Maugham said, "It's a funny thing about life; if you refuse to accept anything but the very best, you very often get it." Champions demand the best from themselves and don't make excuses. They take full responsibility for the results they achieve.

Enjoyment and Oneness. Along with the ease and flow masters display, most enjoy and are totally immersed in their activity, no matter how extreme their effort. Great artists, athletes, and musicians become entirely absorbed in their feats of creation and achievement. They report a sense of timelessness and oneness with their activity, which can be described as "ecstasy."

Commitment and Discipline. True excellence is only achieved through total commitment and consistent discipline. Discipline does not refer to a mindless, mechanical, grim, stiff-jawed approach to learning. Rather, it entails an organized, intelligent, aware, consistent, enthusiastic, unrelenting commitment to a process that leads to the realization of a goal.

In the years that we have been teaching accelerated learning, we have discovered many ways to make the learning process faster and more enjoyable. At the same time, however, our respect for the traditional values of perseverance, commitment, and discipline has only grown deeper. For any meaningful accomplishment, disciplined practice is essential.

So: What does practice make? Perfect? Not necessarily! The key is to practice with a commitment to practicing at the highest level. In the words of the legendary American football coach, Vince Lombardi: "Practice doesn't make perfect. Perfect practice makes perfect!" This phrase emphasizes that continuing practice based on an inaccurate model can make you increasingly less skilled in your chosen areas of endeavor. Understanding the correct models and qualities of excellence provides a key to perfecting your practice. Next, let's focus on how to model these models.

How to See

The key to getting the most out of your observation of models of excellence is to integrate two modes of perception: focused-analytical and open-receptive.

1. FOCUSED-ANALYTICAL.   In this mode of seeing, observe and analyze the technical elements of the performance of those who excel. Study in detail the manifestations of the fundamental elements of their discipline, noting both those things that they do as well as those things they do not.

2. OPEN-RECEPTIVE.   In this mode of seeing, you observe excellence with the eyes of a child. You need not analyze but simply "breathe in" the entire multisensory image, imagining the quality of excellence spreading throughout both your body and mind, becoming part of your own essence. You can think of this way of seeing as nourishment or brain food.

Let's say you have the opportunity to spend a few hours watching the world's greatest juggler. How can you get the most out of your observation? Begin by studying specific elements of the juggler's technique (focused-analytical); note the positioning of the elbows and hands, body posture, facial expression, and breathing rhythm, height and trajectory of the throws, and so on. As you study what the juggler is doing, you're also learning what she is *not* doing: raising shoulders, holding her breath, etc. Then, shift to the open-receptive mode: watch the "whole pattern" of your master juggler. As you watch, allow your body to move in harmony with the juggler's rhythm. Listen to the sounds of the pattern and incorporate them into your overall feeling of excellent juggling.

EXCELLENCE VIDEOS

Of course, until you become one, it's not always practical to have a master juggler around the house. In the meantime, you can nurture your evolving model of excellence by using videotapes. Watch tapes of the greatest performers in your chosen area of endeavor (you may rent, buy, or make your own). Apply both modes of seeing on a regular basis—immersing yourself in brain-nourishing images of excellence!

An interesting subliminal example of this phenomenon on a mass scale takes place each summer in England, when the Wimbledon tennis tournament is shown on television. Tennis coaches around the country report a marked improvement in the performance of their students and club members in the weeks following the tournament. Now we know how to take conscious advantage of this "Wimbledon effect."

In the old days, top collegiate and professional sports teams used to watch game films and point out all the players' errors. While this practice continues into the present, teams have added a new dimension. Now, they watch the game films and catch players "doing something right." Players are encouraged to watch videos of their performance, "doing something right"—over and over—to imprint the image of their high performance onto their minds and bodies.

VISUALIZATION

Your brain is the greatest audio-video producer on the planet, able to produce far more films and shows than have been created in the history of Hollywood! The greats have always used this "internal-vision-scape" to lead them in their chosen destiny. It is a capacity that everyone has, waiting to be used to its potential.

In order to take full advantage of the images of excellence that nourish your brain, you can use your synaesthetic (using all your senses) imagination to create your own internal video replays, with yourself as the star. In these replays it is important to visualize yourself succeeding. Refine your image of perfection and see yourself displaying the qualities of appropriate effort, complete enjoyment, dedicated discipline, ease, and grace.

DOES IT WORK?   A growing body of evidence, from experiments performed by psychologists around the world, shows that visualizing works. One of the classic experiments was conducted by Australian psychologist Alan Richardson:

> Richardson took three groups of people and tested their performance in basketball free-throw shooting. The first group was told to practice every day for twenty minutes. The second group was told to forget about basketball altogether. The third group was told to sit down, relax, and imagine themselves successfully sinking free throws for twenty minutes. Richardson instructed them to feel themselves releasing the ball, see the perfect arc, hear the sound of the

ball swishing through the net, and feel the satisfaction resulting from that imagined success.

At the end of the experimental period, he retested the three groups and found that the first group, the ones that actually practiced each day, had improved their shooting by 24 percent. The second group, who were instructed to completely forget about basketball, had made no improvement. The third group, the ones who were told to "just think about it," improved their shooting percentage by 23 percent.

Other experimenters have replicated Richardson's results, not only in basketball free-throw shooting but also in a wide range of other activities, including dart throwing, ring-tossing, skating, and karate. The conclusion is that visualization, especially when it is multisensory, can produce a marked increase in actual performance.

THE GREAT VISUALIZERS. In addition to experiments previously mentioned, history is rich with great visualizers from all disciplines. John F. Kennedy, the entire American scientific community, and indeed, the American people in the 1960s envisioned a human being setting foot on the moon by the end of the decade. With appropriate effort and discipline, that vision became a reality.

Jack Nicklaus has stated that at the top level of professional golf, 80 percent of success depends on the image of excellence the golfer carries; or in the inimitable words of Yogi Berra, "90 percent of the game is 50 percent mental!"

Muhammad Ali's visualization was so powerful he "injected" his images of success into the minds of his opponents, encouraging them to fall when he said they would. They did. In planting those images, Ali used sound, rhythm, and timing to project to his opponents the sense of *feeling* his punches land, the sound of the fans cheering for him, and so on.

Artists from past to present, from Michelangelo through Picasso to such modern-day artists as Australia's Lorraine Gill, visualize perfect images and then apply dedicated discipline to making those images become a reality. Michelangelo reported "seeing" the image of his sculpture in the stone and simply removing the unnecessary and inappropriate material until only his perfect vision remained. Lorraine Gill, in less than one week of creative visualization, first sees and then sketches an entire series of paintings on the nature of perception. She will then spend the next decade refining the reality on the canvas to coincide with her original vision.

It would be very interesting to record photographically, not the stages of a painting, but its metamorphoses. One would see perhaps by what course a mind finds its way towards the crystallization of its dream. But what is really very serious is to see that the picture does not change basically, that the initial vision remains almost intact. . . . —Pablo Picasso

---

One of our favorite examples of the power of visualization is the saga of Major James Nesmeth. Nesmeth was an average club golfer who regularly shot in the mid-nineties. During a tour of duty in Vietnam he was captured and sent to a prison camp. Living in a tiny cell, isolated from others, Nesmeth was held in terrible conditions for seven years. To maintain his sanity he began practicing visualization, playing eighteen holes of golf in his mind's eye every day. Nesmeth imagined himself on his favorite course, dressed in his favorite outfit. In his mind's eye, he created a vivid sensation of every detail; the sound of the wind blowing through the trees along each fairway, the smell of the freshly cut greens. He savored each step around the course and pictured all the possible shots he might need to make under different weather conditions. For every shot, he chose the appropriate club and felt his hands cradle it with a perfect grip. He imagined the sensation of a perfect swing, listened to the sound of the club making perfect contact with the ball, and then pictured a perfect follow-through. He'd watch the little white orb sail through the air, landing just on the spot where he wanted it to go. When Nesmeth was finally liberated he returned home and went straight to his favorite golf course. He shot a seventy-four, twenty strokes better than his previous average—twenty strokes better, without touching a real club in seven years!

In many other areas, from business to medicine and beyond, stories abound of visionaries and seers who followed their evolving ideal images and, by application and dedication, made them real. Stephen Covey, author of *The 7 Habits of Highly Effective People,* calls this "beginning with the end in mind." Covey emphasizes that all accomplishments are created twice: first in the mind and then in the world.

Most of us visualize on a daily basis, but we often do it unconsciously and in a negative fashion. It is called worrying. What happens to our bodies when we worry? We tense up, disrupt our normal breathing, and psycho-physically prepare ourselves for failure. Instead, learn to use positive visualization to prepare yourself for success. As you do you will transform the energy that supports your worrying into fuel for making your dreams come true.

THE MIND/BODY CONNECTION AND VISUALIZATION.
Visualization works because the mind and body are linked in a profoundly intimate way. Science is just beginning to understand this connection. One of the most fascinating studies was conducted by Dr. John Basmajian of Emory University. Basmajian took extremely fine electrodes and connected them to single motor muscular units in people's forearms. By connecting these electrodes to an oscilloscope and an audio amplifier, Basmajian was able to record the electro-contractile pattern of each motor unit. This unit consisted of one nerve cell and a tiny muscle bundle, and each one showed its own special pattern, unique from the others in both the shape of the spikes on the oscilloscope and in a corresponding "popping" sound recorded on the audio amplifier.

Basmajian then discovered that by just envisioning it, people could change the firing pattern of each individual unit. He went on to report that "most persons became so skilled they could produce a variety of rhythms such as doublets, triplets, galloping rhythms and even complicated drum rolls and drum beats."

The power of visualization can affect individual motor units and change the muscular activity around those cells. Thus, positive, conscious, multisensory visualizations of excellence energize the muscle groups needed to perform an action, subtly tuning the entire mind and body to *appropriate effort* at the time of performance.

TIPS ON VISUALIZATION.   The following thoughts will help you get the most from your visualization practice:

Know You are Equipped. Realize that everyone (including you) can visualize. If you feel you do not have the ability to visualize, ask yourself if you can describe—even roughly—the following objects: your car; an elephant; your home; an apple. Obviously, you can.

These images reside in the occipital lobe of your brain. The occipital lobe acts as your own personal biocomputerized archive, storing billionfold collections of images from your personal history. At this very moment, this part of your brain has the potential to store an infinite series of new images and, in conjunction with your frontal lobes, to create that many more.

Some people naturally see these images vividly while others think that their mind's eye does not offer up clear pictures. The benefits of visualization practice accrue even if you just "think" about your desired goal without seeing technicolor images in your mind's eye.

The ability to picture a desired outcome is built into your brain, and your brain is designed through millions of years of evolution to help you succeed in matching that picture with your performance.

Make Your Visualization Multisensory. The more thoroughly you involve your senses, the more powerful your visualization becomes. As you visualize juggling, for example, imagine the feeling of the shape, texture, and weight of the balls in your hands. See the color of the balls and picture their perfect trajectory. Listen to the rhythmic sounds of a perfect cascade.

Unless you are already a master, your visualization will have gaps in it. Take whatever images you have, and over the days, weeks, months, and years use your models of excellence to furnish your visualization with greater depth and richness.

Practice. Just like any other skill, your ability to visualize will improve with practice. Commit yourself to a regular schedule of mental practice. Some of the best times for practicing visualization include:

- in the morning upon waking
- at night just before you go to bed
- when you are a passenger in a train, plane, boat, or auto
- when taking a break from work
- after meditation, yoga, or exercise, or anytime your body is relaxed and your mind is free.

Visualize Outside-in and Inside-out. When visualizing, imagine that you are watching yourself from the outside. For example, if you are visualizing a ballroom dance routine, watch yourself from the perspective of the judges. Then, "reenter" your body and visualize your perfect dance from the inside out. Then, experiment with merging your inner and outer visualizations!

Distinguish Between Fantasy and Visualization. It's fun to fantasize about being a great juggler, athlete, or millionaire, but fantasizing is not the same as visualizing. A fantasy does not require conscious attention and it is not as focused or energizing as a visualization. Visualization is conscious work. Of course, your fantasies and daydreams may plant the seeds for your visualizations, but dreams only become real as the result of work that takes place first in the mind, then in the world.

Become your vision. "Become" your model of excellence. Many of the great actors, such as Sir Laurence Olivier, Bette Davis, and Marlon Brando, regularly reported being "overcome" by the characters they played. Do that: immerse yourself in images of excellence.

Keep it positive. When doubts, fears, or negative images arise, acknowledge them, and then reinforce your image of success.

WHAT ABOUT REALITY?

Models of excellence and visualization are key ingredients in achieving high performance. Yet without accurate information about our current level of performance, they are incomplete. Many practitioners of New Age positive thinking fall into the trap of one-dimensionality: constantly affirming visions of wonderfulness without honestly assessing reality. They use visualization and affirmations as an escape from reality rather than as a tool to improve it. In order to progress, you must be able to compare your visualization of excellence with your current level of performance.

You need accurate feedback to lead you effectively and efficiently to your goal. Make honest assessments of what you want, and of where you are now. It is essential to see yourself clearly and truly, eliminating subjective fear-based, ego-centered interpretations or misinformation. The potential energy between your present status and your goal creates a positive and dynamic tension, which, when you allow it, will naturally manifest itself in achievement. Many of us have difficulty getting this necessary, accurate information for the following reasons:

SUBJECTIVITY. We live "inside ourselves," so it is difficult to view ourselves from the outside. When learning to juggle, for example, you may *think* that you are throwing the balls up in staggered timing (cascading) when in reality you are handing them across (showering). Frequently, you will remain unaware until you see yourself in a mirror or video, or receive feedback from a partner or a coach.

We use video feedback as a training tool in many of our seminars. Participants are often amazed to discover the discrepancy between their perceptions and the truth the video reveals.

HABIT. Our habitual ways of acting and perceiving can lock us into limiting patterns that start to feel normal. This syndrome was first described by F. M. Alexander, who called it "debauched kinaesthesia."

Alexander observed that when we experience a new, superior, more natural behavior, it often feels *un*natural because our more practiced patterns have become "normal." In other words, right feels wrong because wrong has become normal and *assumed* right! Take, for example, the person who habitually slouches. When adjusted into a fully upright position, the person reports feeling off-balance and about to fall over!

FEAR. Even if accurate information is available, fear will often prevent us from utilizing it appropriately. Many of us grow up with the idea that mistakes are bad, linking our self-esteem with continued successes. We become afraid of making mistakes. So in order to achieve success, we tend to steer clear of areas that may lie outside the apparent realm of our natural talent. In this perverse equation, the secret of success becomes *avoiding failure*, leaving much of our potential untapped.

In order to reach our full potential to learn, we must accept and then transform anxiety and fear, relentlessly seeking accurate information on our performance. What used to be perceived as criticism now becomes a gift for constructive growth.

THE LEARNING SPIRAL

In order to access your full capacity for learning, your brain needs two kinds of information: (1) clear goals and (2) accurate feedback. Both ingredients are essential. If you have a clear vision but inaccurate feedback, you will be deluded, living in a fantasy world. If you have accurate feedback but are without vision, you will be uninspired and stagnant. If you have neither, well . . . you probably wouldn't be reading this book.

The gap between your evolving images of excellence and increasingly pure objective data on your performance energizes the learning process. This creative tension, *embraced with a commitment to success*, results in a continuous, positive spiral, accelerating you toward and beyond your goals.

Your brain is a success mechanism, and this comparison process is its operational secret. As you come to understand and practice it, you will realize that if you choose it, your success in juggling, learning, and life is inevitable.

GUIDELINES FOR EXCELLENCE

- Seek excellent jugglers and videos of their performances to help you form your models of excellence.
- Make visualization an integral part of your juggling practice.
- Visualize synaesthetically (using all your senses), concentrating on the feel of your juggling balls, their color, rhythm, sound: imagine the sensation of the juggling flow state!
- Join the International Jugglers' Association, and attend juggling festivals, where you can immerse yourself in a total juggling experience. (International Jugglers' Association, Box 218, Montague, Massachusetts 01351, USA. (1) 413 367-2401.)
- Practice with playfulness, relish, and joy.
- Take every opportunity to gain objective feedback on your juggling: watch yourself in the mirror; record yourself on video; ask friends for help.
- Be a student of excellence in juggling and in all things. As Plato suggested, "For he (or she) who would proceed aright . . . should begin in youth to visit beautiful forms   out of that he should create fair thoughts; and soon he will of himself perceive that the beauty of one form is akin to the beauty of another, and that beauty in every form is one and the same."
- Create models of excellence in every area of your life: relationships, career, finances, service, hobbies, etc.
- Visualize your goals in life and make sure they all fit together.

- Seek information for improvement in all areas of your life. Ask colleagues, bosses, friends, relatives, coaches, and children for constructive feedback.
- If you want to strengthen the vividness of your multisensory visualization, try the following: Picture your favorite scene—enjoy some deep full breaths and then close your eyes. Create a picture of your favorite place. Perhaps, for example, you choose a beach. In your mind's eye look out at the vast expanse of the blue-green ocean and enjoy the foamy white wavecrests. Listen to the sound of the surf and feel the rays of the sun on your back. Breathe in the invigorating smell of the salty air and feel the texture of the sand underfoot. Follow the soaring flight path of a white gull against the clear blue sky. Pick up a handful of sand and let it fall through your fingers, watching the light dance off the crystals. Continue enjoying your visit to your favorite place, relishing every delightful detail!
- Try the fruition exercise: Assemble as many of the following fruits as you can: a red apple, an orange, a lemon, a bunch of green and/or purple grapes, a handful of blueberries. Place them on a table in front of you and sit quietly for a few moments, following the flow of your breathing to help you relax. Then, look at the apple carefully, studying its shape and color for about thirty seconds. Now, close your eyes and re-create this image in your mind's eye. Do the same with each of the fruits in turn. Then repeat the exercise, only this time hold the apple in your hands as you study it. Inhale its aroma and take a big bite. Bring your full attention to the taste, smell, and texture of your juicy apple. When you have swallowed your bite, close your eyes and see the apple, enjoying all the luscious multisen-

sory associations. After you have sampled each fruit (don't take a big bite of your lemon, a little nibble will do the trick), picture each one in your mind's eye. Then, in your imagination, create a picture of each fruit magnified 100 times. Shrink the fruits back to regular size and imagine viewing them from different angles. Then imagine the fruits dancing in the juggler's box in front of you.

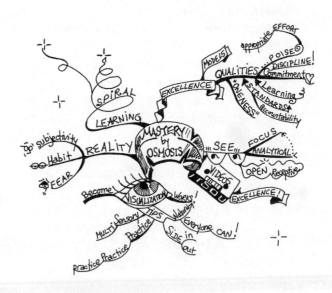

4

. . .

FAILURE AS SUCCESS:

LEARNING TO LOVE YOUR

MISTAKES

A man's errors are his portals of discovery.

—JAMES JOYCE

Once, when Tony had just passed his first juggulation stage and was making himself tense trying too hard to be perfect, he threw one of the balls too high. It hit the ground hard and bounced far above his head. Then, in a moment of wonder, he relaxed and watched the ball land perfectly in his hand, falling into the juggling flow state. This serendipitous "error" soon became one of his favorite regular tricks, and now, whenever he drops the balls, he looks for another "error master-piece."

YOUR BRAIN IS BETTER THAN YOU THINK!

In the last chapter we emphasized the power of multidimensional visions of excellence for tapping our vast potential to learn. Of course, in order to make our visions come true we have to practice . . . and practicing involves making mistakes!

Many of us grow up thinking of mistakes as bad, viewing errors as evidence of fundamental incapacity. This negative thinking pattern can create a self-fulfilling prophecy, which undermines the learning process. To maximize our learning it is essential to ask: "How can we get the most from every mistake we make?"

Ironically, our willingness to do this often depends on our level of confidence in our ability. Many people pay lip service to the idea of learning from mistakes while avoiding new learning opportunities.

Confidence in one's ability to learn from mistakes builds success, and success builds more confidence. Develop confidence in your learning ability by cultivating a practical appreciation of the amazing capacity of your brain.

One of the most inspiring pieces of research into the brain's capacity was done by Professor Pyotr Anokhin of Moscow University in the early 1970s. Professor Anokhin, a student of Pavlov, spent the last ten years of his life investigating the nature of the brain cell, the specific nature of the synapse (the area where brain cells connect), and the number of possible thought patterns that each human brain could make. His estimates staggered the entire scientific community. He established that the minimum number of patterns your brain can make is the number "1" followed by 10.5 million kilometers of typewritten zeros. Anokhin said it is as if the human brain were "a multidimensional musical instrument that could play an infinite number of musical pieces simultaneously." Anokhin further stated that no man or woman, past or present, had even begun to truly explore the full potential of the brain.

Anokhin's work represented the beginning of an explosion of interest in understanding the nature and capacity of the brain. Biologists, chemists, physicists, psychologists, philosophers, and computer scientists are increasingly focusing their attention on the brain, inspiring the U.S. Congress to declare the 1990s the "Decade of the Brain."

Nearly 95 percent of what we know about the brain has been discovered in the past 10 years. We are just beginning to apply that knowledge to the practical business of learning how to learn.

In the 1950s it was assumed that we use 50 percent of our brain's potential. In the 1960s estimates dropped, suggesting we use only 10 percent. In the 1970s and 1980s estimates dropped further, to 1 percent, and now, in the 1990s, many brain researchers are convinced that we use less than .01 percent of our brain's capacity. So, either we are all getting dimmer or our brain's potential is far greater than we imagined. The news is good: the potential of your brain is far greater than had ever been thought, and even now we are probably underestimating its true capacity.

Each of us is gifted with a birthright of virtually unlimited potential. Our greatest fulfillment lies in the process of expressing our gift. Your brain is the most profoundly powerful learning mechanism in all known creation. The next time you are faced with a learning challenge, remember that you possess a magnificent biocomputer designed to learn and create—designed to guarantee your success.

TRIAL AND ERROR—TRIAL AND SUCCESS

Targeted by visualization, the tremendous capacity of your brain is unleashed by embracing the process of trial and error. In the words of Buckminster Fuller, "the human brain is a trial-and-error mechanism." And both we and Fuller agree that the word *error* describes a process designed to ensure *success*.

Fuller emphasized that to achieve full expression, we must continually experiment, focusing equal attention on successes and failures. The path to accelerating and enjoying the learning *process* requires us to see success and failure as equally instructive and valuable.

It is useful to view any learning experience—juggling in this case—as a fascinating, never-ending journey from a starting point toward your continually evolving goal of excellence. A typical pathway is shown in the illustration on page 73.

First, the brain focuses on its goal. It aims, makes its first attempt, and ends up at point one: off-center, away from the goal. This is traditionally considered an "error," "mistake," or "failure." Actually, the brain has progressed toward its goal. It now has all the data it originally had, and it has *new* information from the first attempt.

On the second, third, and fourth attempts, similar errors and failures occur. Instead of thinking of these as mistakes, view them as further additions to the data bank of understanding; they are an integral part of learning. Chinese martial artists call this "investing in

loss." These investments enable us to accelerate our
rate of learning return.

Sometimes, despite our best efforts, we find ourselves stuck on a plateau or apparently getting worse.
These points in the learning process, inevitably experienced by every individual, are danger points. This is
when frustration can lead to feelings of hopelessness,
despair, and fundamental inadequacy, causing many
people to give up.

In every country every language has its own phrases
reserved for this point in the learning process. Classics
include, "I can't," "See, I told you I was no good," "I
knew it was impossible," "I've never been very good at
this sort of thing," "Perhaps I should try something
else," "I stink," "I'll never get this," "Either you've got
it or you don't and I don't," and so on.

If you find yourself at one of these points in your
learning or life, you must:

1. Understand and accept your current reality, seeking accurate feedback on your performance.
2. Refine and then vivify your vision of excellence.
3. Remember the vast power of your brain, your limitless capacity to learn, and recognize that a drop in
performance is not a sign of fundamental incapacity,
but rather, an integral part of your natural path to
improvement.
4. Carry on.

Your Brain as Auto-Pilot

The process of succeeding can be seen as a series of
trials in which your vision constantly guides you toward
your target while in your actual performance you are

regularly slightly off target. Success in any area requires constantly readjusting your behavior as the result of feedback from your experience.

"I've never been afraid to fail."—Michael Jordan at a news conference announcing his desire to play professional baseball for the Chicago White Sox.

You can think of this process as similar to the auto-pilot on airplanes. In a flight from Florida to London, the airplane is actually off course 93 percent of the time. Onboard computers monitor the variables of wind, pressure, altitude, temperature, speed, and air traffic, and adjust the flight path accordingly.

When you are committed to a clearly envisioned goal, your brain will act like an auto-pilot, steering your perception and behavior toward success. Even though you may seem to be stuck on a plateau, your brain will be doing the connecting and interrelating that is necessary on a subconscious level. Then, when your mind and body are ready, you will make the next leap forward.

This process continues throughout life: when you have reached one goal, you will have learned to enjoy the process so much that you'll want to reach for the next horizon. You will eventually pursue new goals, new dimensions, new vistas, and—like a baby—delight in the process as much or even more than in the goal. When you have reached this stage, you will have realized that success and failure are like the two sides of the Möbius strip. They appear different, yet are fundamentally the same.

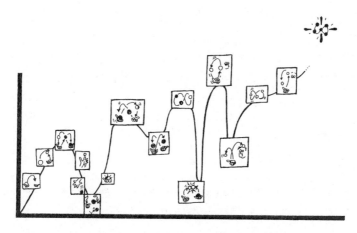

INDIVIDUAL GRAPH OF PROGRESS

YOUR UNIQUE PATTERN

Looking again at the graph of individual progress, we can see that while each individual's graph is unique, all contain the fundamental elements of (1) successes, (2) failures, and (3) plateaus. The general pattern of your graph will be *toward success*, and your own individual progress toward that success will incorporate all the ups and downs of your natural learning rhythm.

Your graph of progress applies not only to your juggling program but also to any activity in which you choose to engage—be it a sport, music, academics, art,

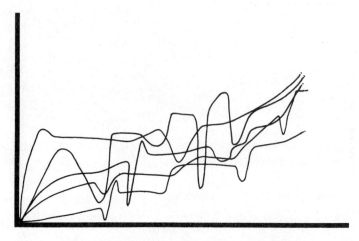

MANY INDIVIDUAL GRAPHS OF PROGRESS

the development of your personal relationships, your pathway through life.

A common pitfall on the path of excellence is an overemphasis on comparing our progress with others. While competition can be a tremendous tool for stretching ourselves to new heights, too often it causes a loss of perspective. This loss of perspective can often be traced to the following cycle: losing becomes associated with failure, and failure with the loss of self-esteem.

Winning becomes a matter of proving one's worth rather than a by-product of full self-expression. This distorted view often results in a mania for winning or an avoidance of healthy competition. "Losing" is a form of feedback on the state of your current reality. It provides a wealth of opportunity for you to grow in your own "graph of progress." "Winning" means it's time to set a higher goal.

GREATNESS

The greats often became great because they continued to believe in themselves despite apparent failures. The history of achievement in every field is a chronicle of overcoming adversity and learning from mistakes:

- Thomas Edison failed thousands of times in his attempt to invent the light bulb. After his experiments blew up three laboratories, his friends urged him to try something else. Edison replied that as the result of his errors he now knew more than ever and that his success was inevitable. Thousands of trials resulting in errors created a knowledge base that propelled him to success.
- Abraham Lincoln failed in business twice by age twenty-four. He lost numerous elections and had a nervous breakdown before being elected President of the United States at age fifty-two. Lincoln incorporated the lessons learned from adversity to become a wise statesman and visionary leader.
- When Einstein's father asked Albert's schoolmaster what career path his son should follow, the teacher replied, "It does not matter, he will never make a succees of anything." Gregor Mendel, originator of the modern science of genetics, flunked biology. Winston Churchill, Charles Darwin, W. B. Yeats, Hans Christian Andersen, General George Patton,

Gustave Flaubert, and Leonardo da Vinci all experienced problems in school on their paths to greatness.

• Walt Hriniak, batting coach of baseball's Chicago White Sox, points out that the critical distinguishing characteristic of the great batters is their ability to deal with mistakes. In his own inimitable words, "I don't care who you are, if you're one of the great stars of all time, making millions of dollars or some Little League kid, someday you're gonna stink." Hriniak emphasizes that all the greats have, at one time or another, experienced a major batting slump. He states that "the ability to learn and maintain a good attitude when things aren't going your way" is the key to breaking out of a slump. Hriniak emphasizes that even the greatest hitters fail in 60 to 70 percent of their trips to the plate. Yet, they approach every opportunity with a total commitment to success.

This approach to greatness applies to organizations as well as individuals.

The manager of the future will simply be a learning guide.
—*Peter Drucker*

The most successful corporation of the 1990s will be something called a learning organization.—Fortune *magazine*

Most Fortune 500 companies, for example, have profit patterns reflecting medium success, followed by products with astounding success, followed by major failures, followed by medium success, followed by smaller failures, and so on. A significant percentage of companies drop out of the 500 every year, and over a twenty-year period more than 30 percent go out of business altogether. The best companies demonstrate an overall trend toward improvement, integration, and growth. What's the key difference between the organizations that fall by the wayside and those that continue? The ability to learn from their failures and creatively adapt to unpredictable circumstances.

Soichiro Honda, founder of Honda Motors, credits his phenomenal success to a high tolerance for failure. He says, "Many people dream of success. To me, success can only be achieved through repeated failure and introspection."

The ability to learn and adapt in the face of "failure" provides businesses with a critical competitive advantage. The best organizations build environments that support risk-taking and a creative approach to failure. Johnson & Johnson, for example, is renowned for its innovative business practices and quality products. The tone for this success was set by the company's founder, General Johnson. CEO James Burke, in an interview with leadership guru Warren Bennis, said:

> "I once developed a new product that failed badly, and General Johnson called me in, and I was sure

he was going to fire me. . . . Johnson said to me, 'I understand you lost over a million dollars.' . . . I said, 'Yes sir. That's correct.' So he stood up and held out his hand. He said, 'I just want to congratulate you. All business is making decisions, and if you don't make decisions, you won't have any failures. The hardest job I have is getting people to make decisions. If you make that same decision wrong again, I'll fire you. But I hope you'll make a lot of others, and that you'll understand there are going to be more failures than successes.'"

According to Bennis, leadership can't flourish without a positive attitude to learning and mistakes. To be truly successful organizations must, he emphasizes, view mistakes as a normal part of the quest for excellence. Organizations that create healthy learning environments are those where all individuals, *beginning at the top*, take responsibility for acknowledging, correcting, and learning from their own mistakes.

In the 1980s Johnson & Johnson was rocked by the infamous Tylenol scandal. A few packages of Tylenol were laced with cyanide by a madman intent on defaming the company. When a consumer died as a result and the story hit the front pages, bedlam ensued. Johnson & Johnson's sales and profits dropped markedly. How did the company react? They temporarily took the product off the market, reassuring customers by launching a full investigation of the tampering. They did not try to cover up or obfuscate the issue. They reintroduced the product with tamper-proof packaging. Sales and profits returned to previous levels, and consumer attitudes toward the company actually improved!

Unfortunately, Johnson & Johnson is unusual. In

most organizations the fear of failure remains the dominant motivating force in everyday life. In a fascinating study of the decision dynamics of major pension funds, for example, researchers discovered that investment decisions were not based primarily on ensuring the best possible return for the funds, but rather, they were consistently made in such a way as to minimize the "blameability" of individual investment managers. A major study of inefficiency and waste at the IRS concluded that the overwhelming cause of the problems was the unwillingness, at most levels of the organization, to acknowledge and correct mistakes.

The unwillingness to acknowledge and learn from mistakes is the source of many of our society's greatest problems. Watergate, Irangate, the Savings and Loan debacle, all were made dramatically worse by attempted cover-ups. Our growth as individuals and as a society requires us to transform our attitude toward mistakes. One way to begin is to learn to make them on purpose.

Stick to it! On a daily basis, put a Post-it Note on your desk, telephone, or computer and write yourself an inspiring message, perhaps one of your favorite quotes or a reminder to act on one of your goals. The Post-it Note itself provides inspiration. The product was born from the failure of 3M company researchers to produce a strong new bonding compound. Instead of throwing it out and firing those responsible, management encouraged people to discover what could be learned from this apparent fiasco. In a classic story of snatching success from the jaws of failure, associates noticed that the "failed" product was ideal for "posting" temporary memos. The result? A new staple of office life and millions of dollars for 3M!

MISTAKES ON PURPOSE

When you begin to learn to juggle, it's guaranteed that you will drop the balls whether you plan to or not. You will recall that a key element of our approach to learning to juggle involves consciously dropping the balls. By simplifying the task, and focusing purely on the throw, you learn more from every drop. The result is that you learn to juggle faster, with greater pleasure, *and* you become a better juggler because right from the beginning you are practicing with poise.

When learning something new, try to anticipate mistakes. For example, when learning to drive a standard shift car, most people become quite stressed when the car stalls, as it frequently will. This is particularly upsetting on a hill in heavy traffic. Instead, take the car to an empty parking lot and practice stalling. Discover what too much pressure on the gas pedal feels like. Explore the sensation of too little clutch. As you stall, relax. You will be calibrating your sensitivity and developing greater control. A brief period of practicing this mistake on purpose will result in a much safer and more enjoyable driving experience when you take to the road.

The road to excellence in the martial arts begins with an emphasis on learning how to fall and how to lose. Martial artists know that if you are not comfortable falling, then your stance and balance will be weak. If you don't know how to be thrown, how to lose, you'll never be able to properly execute a throw.

Similarly, in high-wire walking it is essential to begin by learning to relax when you fall. The relaxation allows you to develop the poise to stay up when you lose your balance.

Of course, tightrope walkers practice with a safety net, martial artists use a mat, and new drivers should use a big, empty lot. Whether learning to fall or learning to stall, we learn best when we can practice making mistakes in a safe environment.

Then, in the real world mistakes are less likely.

If you want to succeed, double your failure rate.
—*Thomas Watson, founder of IBM*

HIGHER-LEVEL MISTAKES

After you've dropped the balls for the thousandth time, you may find that they start landing in your hands consistently. But perhaps you now wish to learn four balls. Or the famous "behind the back" trick. (See Chapter 8,"Beyond Infinity.") Guess what's going to start happening again? That's right! If you want to reach a higher level, the balls will have to drop again. After you've mastered four balls, you'll probably want to learn five. Guess what? The balls will drop as you've never seen them drop before.

Aware of your brain's tremendous potential and of the innate *success orientation* of your mind's true design, you can now see your mistakes and failures in a new light—as an integral part of your continuous process of improvement. To continue learning is to embrace the process of trial and error at higher and higher levels.

GUIDELINES FOR SUCCESS

- Practice dropping the balls *intentionally*.
- When the balls drop, watch where they land and adjust your throws accordingly.
- Experience the freedom of "letting go" as you focus on the throw.
- Practice making your mistakes the basis for new creative patterns in your juggling.
- Observe your attitude toward your mistakes. How do you coach yourself when you experience a setback?
- Think of the last three major mistakes you've made in your life. What have you learned from them?
- Whenever learning something new, anticipate mistakes and make them consciously, in a safe environment. Explore them with relish.
- Set clear goals and be sure to enjoy the process of achieving them because "there is no there when you get there." The process of learning continues throughout life, so enjoy moving to higher levels of chaos.
- Start a movement to have your company reorganize the training department, incorporating a positive approach to learning from mistakes: start by suggesting that it be renamed "The Department for Constructive Mistake Making."

5

OLD DOGS, NEW TRICKS

The illiterate of the year 2000 will not be the individual who cannot read and write, but the one who cannot learn, unlearn and relearn.

—ALVIN TOFFLER

In one of our seminars, a student said he couldn't juggle because he was too old. In addition to a history of lacking "ball sense," he reported that "maybe I'm not a juggling kind of guy." We suggested that maybe he *was* a juggling kind of guy. And that perhaps he should start by pretending he was the world's greatest one-ball juggler.

For the first day of the course, he decided to concentrate on perfecting his one-ball technique with a confident mental attitude. On the morning of the second day, he progressed to throwing and dropping two balls. By that afternoon, he was dropping three balls with panache. Having outwitted his habits, the balls started landing in his hands—almost as if by accident. Much to his delight, he completed his first juggulation.

BRAIN AND AGE

What happens to your brain as you get older? Many people assume that mental and physical abilities necessarily decline with age, that we are, after age twenty-five, losing significant brain capacity on a daily basis.

In reality, the average brain is capable of improving with age. Our neurons are capable of making increasingly complex new connections throughout our lives. And our neuronal endowment is so great that even if we lost 1,000 brain cells every day for the rest of our lives, it would still be less than 1 percent of our total (of course it's important not to lose the 1 percent that you actually use).

Why is it then that so many people do seem to get worse? In a nutshell the answer is habits—habits of thinking and doing. As we age, it becomes all too easy to get stuck in a routine. And often, our routine is accompanied by an assumption that education ends when we finish school, and that our mental and physical performance will inevitably decline.

Moreover, when most of us went to school we had little choice regarding the subjects we were supposed to learn. Whether it was singing, drawing, sports, or maths class, almost everyone experienced the embarrassment of having to perform publicly in an area in which they were unskilled. As adults we can usually avoid the discomfort and embarrassment associated with learning something unfamiliar because we have more choice regarding what we do and what we learn. Most grown-ups choose to focus only on those areas in which they have obvious natural talent and avoid the subjects that were sources of embarrassment in school. Schooling conditions many of us to avoid the new, the challenging, the unfamiliar. As a result, many people become narrower in their perspective as they get older.

The most recent research into aging and human performance suggests that like Goethe, Verdi, Bertrand Russell, Georgia O'Keeffe, Pablo Picasso, Mstislav Rostropovich, Martha Graham, George Foreman, Nolan Ryan, George Burns, and Chateau Mouton Rothschild, most of us have the ability to improve with age. The key to this continuous improvement lies in nurturing a positive attitude toward aging, while regularly challenging habits—stretching our minds and bodies—with new learning activities.

Of course, we need our habits. Life would be inconvenient without them. You don't want to have to perform a creative exercise every morning to find a new way to brush your teeth or tie your shoes. However, when you do want to change something, it is important to know how. Let's explore the way our brains form habits so that we can learn how to change them when we choose.

HABITS AS BRAIN GROOVES

Each one of your brain cells is like a tiny octopus with a center and many tentacles. Each of these tentacles has hundreds of thousands of connection points called *dendritic spines*. Dendritic spines look like little mushrooms and are the connection points between your billions of brain cells. Each brain cell wraps its tentacles around the tentacles of up to as many as 10,000 other brain cells, delicately linking the multiple billions of little mushrooms. The place where the mushrooms meet is called the synapse.

The way your brain functions can be understood as follows: an electrical impulse passes down one arm of a brain cell and at a given instant triggers a chemical reaction in one particular dendritic spine. These chemicals travel across the synaptic gap and stimulate the chemicals in the opposite dendritic spine, which in turn trigger an electrical response that travels down the branch of the receiving brain cell. This process is repeated down the line of links, forming a patterned pathway called a *trace*.

These intricate patterns are the building blocks of your learning, your memory, and all your habits. If any learned information, memory, or habit is repeated, the same pattern of electrical and chemical activity repeats itself in your brain. Each repetition makes it easier for the electrical and chemical responses to travel down the pathway. It is much like a walk through a jungle—the first time you have to hack your way through. Your progress is impeded because you have to clear away undergrowth. The second time you travel that same path it becomes easier; the third time, even more so . . . until it becomes a clear path.

As Anokhin confirmed, your brain has the potential to make 1 followed by 10.5 million kilometers of zeros' worth of patterns. This suggests that your capacity for learning, for memorization, for creating and establishing new habits, is virtually infinite.

Why, with this infinite capacity, do so many of us get stuck in apparently unchangeable habit patterns? Having established a habit—positive or negative—that habit is likely to dominate your behavior until a new, stronger, habit is "grooved." Changing habits requires consciously "rewiring" our brain. How is this done?

IT BEGINS WITH AWARENESS

How many gurus, master teachers, therapists, and coaches does it take to change a light bulb? Only one, but the light bulb has to want to change. Of course, before the light bulb can want to change it must know that it needs to change.

As you recall from chapter 2, many people get stuck in the habit of passing balls directly across the bottom of the box, rather than throwing the balls to the top (showering instead of cascading). In most cases, people who do this think they are cascading, when in reality, they are showering. After they see themselves in a mirror or a video, or receive feedback from a partner or coach, they begin to be able to recognize the deviant pattern.

In the movie *Awakenings*, Robert DeNiro plays an inmate of a psychiatric institution. In an interview with the governing board of psychiatrists, he is asked, "Are you aware of the unconscious gestures of hostility you are making toward this board?" to which DeNiro's character replies, "If they are unconscious, how could I be aware of them?"

Before we can change a habit or behavior, we must bring it to consciousness. The first step in the change process is awareness.

Having brought a habit to consciousness, we can then access our capacity for inhibition. Not inhibition in the Freudian sense; rather the neuromuscular equivalent of saying no. Before you can throw the balls in a cascade, you must stop the showering pattern. You will recall that in order to change the habit of showering, we recommend that you throw the first ball and then *pause*.

The pause allows you to inhibit the activity of the old neuromuscular pathways responsible for your habit.

You are now ready to build new neuromuscular pathways based on visualizations you create from a coach's instructions, internalizations of models of excellence, or your own best guess of what might work better. The clearer and more multidimensional your vision, the easier it is to build a new path.

Awareness, inhibition, and visualization are necessary ingredients in the process of change, but they remain insufficient without the power of commitment. Commitment is the cornerstone of creative change. Its power is beautifully expressed in the following quote from Goethe:

> *Until one is committed, there is hesitancy, the chance to draw back, always ineffectiveness. Concerning all acts of initiative (and creation), there is one elementary truth, the ignorance of which kills countless ideas and splendid plans: that the moment one definitely commits oneself, then Providence moves too. All sorts of things occur to help one that would never otherwise have occurred. A whole stream of events issues from the decision, raising in one's favor all manner of unforeseen incidents and meetings and material assistance, which no man could have dreamed would have come his way.*
>
> *Whatever you can do or dream you can, begin it.*
> *Boldness has genius, power, and magic in it.*
> *Begin it now.*

DETOURS ON THE PATH

A common pitfall in the process of change is the illusion of creating new pathways while reinforcing old. We call this phenomenon "false positive thinking." This form of thinking is subtle and dangerous.

A classic illustration is the case of the professional golfer who, on the fifth tee of a major championship, drove his ball into a waterhole four consecutive times. The event became both a joke and focus of attention, with journalists constantly asking him what he was going to do about it. He replied that he would make sure *not to do it* the following year. Then, when he arrived twelve months later, the media couldn't wait to interview him about his thoughts on the fifth tee.

The golfer replied that he had spent a year thinking positively about not repeating his terrible performance, confidently approached the fifth tee, and . . . drove his ball more precisely into the waterhole than he had done on the previous four occasions! Why? While he had been assuming that he was thinking positively, he'd spent his entire year focusing on *not* going into the waterhole, but he had been constantly and competently visualizing the four times he had driven his ball into the waterhole. Under the illusion that he was exercising positive thinking, he had been practicing negative thinking . . . and succeeded brilliantly.

Success in change requires that rather than thinking "I will *not* do what I do *not* want to do," you must think "I will do what I *do* want to do." In the case of the golfer, rather than focusing on his mistake, which he succeeded in replicating, he should have focused on the green of the fifth hole, the feeling of the perfect stroke, and the ideal flight pattern of the ball into the hole, thereby charting the appropriate neuromuscular pathways.

Your intention creates neuromuscular connections, and you have a choice about the quality of connections you create. As you combine commitment, awareness, inhibition, and appropriately positive visualization, *you are awakening and literally re-creating your own brain.*

YOU CAN CHANGE

Our human saga is filled with dramatic examples of people who, even in the face of apparently insurmountable odds, accomplished major changes in their lives. Medical history, for example, is filled with cases of terminally ill patients who've healed themselves by invoking the brain's power.

In *Anatomy of an Illness*, Norman Cousins describes his reaction to being told by his doctor that he had six months to live. Rather than resigning himself to death in a hospital, Cousins moved to a hotel room. There he brought in a film projector and watched funny movies, read humorous stories, and made himself laugh. He meditated, ate a healthy diet and practiced thinking positively. Defying his "death sentence," he lived and went on to write a number of bestselling books on the power of self-healing.

Of course, it is possible to have a positive attitude and still die. As a matter of fact, we can guarantee it. However, in all the stories of dramatic recovery and change against the odds we have studied, one factor remains consistent: a total commitment to change.

Juggler Kit Summers provides an uplifting example. In 1977 he placed first in a nationally televised talent

show. He set a world record by juggling seven clubs
thirty times and in 1979 became the juggling coach for
the Ringling Brothers circus. By 1982 he was starring
on stage at a major casino. And then, while crossing the
street on the way to work, he was hit by a truck. After
thirty-seven days in a coma he awoke to discover that
he couldn't walk, talk, feed himself, and, worst of all,
he couldn't juggle. With amazing patience, dedication,
and discipline Kit set out on the arduous road to recovery. On the one-year anniversary of his accident Kit
performed in public, and although his skill hadn't quite
returned to its previous level, he was on his way to
regaining his stature as one of the best jugglers in the
world. Kit has also become a world-class motivational
speaker and a successful author. His secret? Total commitment, belief in himself, and step-by-step goal setting.

On the evening of his return to performing Kit's
friends threw a "We are glad we are all alive" party in
his honor. Celebrate being alive every day. Live your
highest aspirations; learn what you have always wanted
to learn. Don't wait until you get hit by a truck or acquire a terminal illness to change the things that prevent you from living your life to the full. Whatever your
habits, whatever your age, you can change . . . you can
learn.

GUIDELINES FOR CHANGE

- Commit yourself to the process of growth and continuous improvement. Plan to improve with age.
- Learn something new every day.
- George Burns said that the secret of living a long,
happy life is to do what you love. Commit yourself

to discovering what you love and do it. Then, find a way to get paid for it.

• Keep fit. Much of what passes for senility is a depletion of oxygen to the brain. This depletion is frequently caused by years of sedentary behavior and poor dietary habits. As arteries clog, blood flow to the brain declines. Blood carries the oxygen your brain needs to make new connections. In a fascinating experiment, a group of older people were given an intelligence test, after which they spent fifteen minutes in an oxygen tent. Retested after the oxygen exposure, their intelligence scores improved significantly! To continue the growth of your learning power throughout life, be sure to keep your brain oxygenated by eating well and exercising regularly.

• Live your dreams.

• Find a habit that you'd like to change. (Hint: start with a simple habit such as saying "um" or "you know" when you speak.) Commit to change it. Practice awareness, inhibition, and visualization.

• Be on the lookout for detours on your path. Watch for negative thinking patterns and reframe them positively.

• Perhaps you've noticed that as you get older, time seems to go faster. So, whatever it is that you've always wanted to learn, begin it now—you'll be good at it before you know it.

6

•
• •

THE ART OF
RELAXED CONCENTRATION

When we announce in our juggling classes that we are
about to teach three-ball juggling, people often ask,
"How can I even contemplate three when I don't feel
competent with two?" As they *think* about juggling
three they tend to tighten their bodies and hold their
breath. In this fear state, three-ball juggling is virtually
impossible. The idea that something is going to be difficult is often enough to make it so.

When this happens, we ask the class to bring their
awareness to their breathing and body/mind state. They
are often amazed to discover how much a simple
thought has caused them to contract. We point out that
their fear-based "psychophysical preconception" has
become a negative self-fulfilling prophecy.

Then, we announce that we will give them a second
chance, an opportunity to avoid this pattern and approach three-ball juggling with an attitude of relaxed
concentration. So we make the announcement again.
"Ahem, we are about to learn three balls." The class
usually reacts with laughter and enthusiastic cries of

"Great!" "How 'bout four balls?" "Bring on the chain saws and flaming clubs!" And although it seems silly, postures open, eyes come alive, breathing becomes fuller and freer, and the class is prepared to succeed.

YOU'VE GOT RHYTHM

The natural quality of life is a rhythmic pattern of contraction and expansion, an essential pulsation that can be witnessed clearly in the simple amoeba. If the amoeba is poked, disturbed, or interfered with, there is an immediate contraction and rigidification, and the natural pulsation diminishes. Returned to ideal conditions, the amoeba recommences its natural rhythm. If the amoeba is continually disturbed, however, its healthy pulsation ceases.

This fundamental pattern is present in all members of the animal kingdom, including human beings. A healthy human baby manifests this essential pulsation. Breathing freely, its supple movements and unarmored eyes project a radiant aliveness, a natural quality of relaxed concentration. This quality supports a sense of wonder and fearless curiosity that allows the baby to learn at an incredible rate.

What happens to this freedom, openness, and passion for learning? It is compromised and often stifled by fear. The fear of failure (and success); fear of the unknown; fear of ridicule, embarrassment, humiliation; fear of rejection and the loss of love

These fears affect us physically and psychologically, undermining our natural mind/body coordination and impeding our ability to learn. To reawaken our natural high-performance state of relaxed concentration, it is necessary to transform the energy of fear. Let's begin by understanding the sources of fear and the mechanisms through which it operates.

LEARNING FEAR

PARENTAL TRANSFERENCE.   Babies are natural mimes. They imitate Mommy and Daddy. Their sensitivity and receptiveness are such that they will respond not only to words and sounds but also to the cellular patterns of locked-in fear and tension that often influence parents' behavior.

A common example of fear transference occurs when a baby is learning to walk. Masters of trial-and-error learning, babies fall repeatedly. They do it in a relaxed, almost comfortable manner, making it unlikely that they will be harmed. Anxious parents, however, often induce shock or fear reactions in the child by communicating their own fear about what the baby is doing ("Oh my God, you *will* hurt yourself!").

Another common cause of fear transference is parents' overanxious attempts to socialize their children, to produce "nice little boys and girls." One recent study found that the average child hears the commands "no," "don't," or other negative instructions at least 400 times per day. This overly negative programming takes its toll, interfering with the spontaneity and joy of the learning process.

SCHOOL.   Despite the negative reinforcement that many children receive at home, they often arrive at school in reasonable shape. Most first graders manifest a natural curiosity and openness that is reflected in an effortless, upright, alert posture. By second or third grade, however, one can witness a notable decline in poise. Hunched shoulders and tense faces become more common with each year in school, so that by the time most students reach high school their bodies are both slumped and tense. This decline is partly a function of adjusting to a growing body while having to sit in one place for a long time, day after day, year after year. But the greatest cause of the loss of natural poise is the fear of failure and embarrassment that is the hallmark of our academic process. Think back to first or second grade. Can you recall a time when the teacher asked a question and one of the children in your class waved a hand wildly, exclaiming something like "Ooh, ooh, please call on me—I know!" then blurted out a truly original, creative answer. But on that day the teacher said, "No! Wrong! That's not the answer I was looking for!" And all the kids in the class started laughing, "Ha ha ha . . . what an idiot!" And a little voice in the student's mind said "Never, ever, ever do that again!"

Most of us learn that the game of school is not about self-expression, originality, or creativity. Rather it's about getting the right answer, pleasing authority, and avoiding the humiliation and ostracism associated with failing.

This fear of failure results in a tendency to avoid activities or subjects that do not come easily. We call this the "I can't" phenomenon, and we have observed it around the world. The "I can't" creates a negative, psycho-physical, self-fulfilling prophecy—mind and body conspiring to ensure failure. A typical example is the story of how one of our students developed an "I can't" associated with singing:

"It was choir day at school and all the kids were singing happily. Suddenly the teacher stopped the class and pointed out that someone was singing off-key. We were all told that every single one of us would have to come up to the front of the classroom and sing a few bars solo so that the guilty child could be identified. When my turn came I was terrified. All I remember is feeling as if I were choking as I made a horrible screeching noise and all the other kids started laughing. I've never sung since then. Every time I even think about singing I seize up."

Other classic "I can'ts" include: I can't draw, dance, do mathematics, get organized, be creative, do public speaking (according to *The Book of Lists*, public speaking is the number-one fear of the American and British populations, ranking higher than nuclear war or financial ruin!). Other insidious "I can'ts" include: I can't be happy, make enough money, get along with my spouse, and, believe it or not—juggle!

"I can'ts" are so insidious because they are locked into the body as well as the mind. They sabotage our natural poise and the attitude of relaxed concentration that accompanies it. To rediscover fully our birthright of relaxed concentration, we must find a way to free ourselves from the psycho-physical effects of our "I can't" habits. We are better able to do this as we gain a deeper understanding of the ways fear affects the body and mind.

MECHANISMS OF FEAR

What happens in your mind and body when you are afraid? The following research will help you understand the mechanisms of the fear response.

THE STARTLE PATTERN. Dr. Frank Pierce Jones of Tufts University's Institute for Psychological Research performed an experiment in which he asked 1,000 people to stand, one at a time, in their most comfortable, erect posture. Jones wired each subject with electromyographical equipment, simultaneously setting up a series of stroboscopic cameras in order to measure and monitor people's reactions to an unexpected, loud noise. He found that every subject reacted to the fear stimulus in a virtually identical manner. The reaction involved blinking the eyes, stiffening the neck muscles, holding the breath, and contracting the major joint surfaces of the body.

Jones called this reaction the "startle pattern" and in his subsequent research confirmed that it was a universal reaction to fear. Jones noted that worry, vague apprehensions, anxiety, and depression manifested similarly, but in a slower, more insidious manner. Jones observed, as have the authors, that most people live every day in a modified version of the startle pattern— we tend to become psycho-physically predisposed to react fearfully.

LOSS OF THE BALANCED RESTING STATE. In his original study of cats, which he later generalized to all mammals, Rudolf Magnus observed that cats spend much of their time in what he called the "balanced resting state." The balanced resting state is characterized by the integration of relaxation with readiness for action.

Magnus observed that when a cat sees a mouse, it instantly turns it heads toward it, preparing in a completely coordinated fashion, for a strike. Magnus termed this movement the "attitudinal reflex." Magnus observed that if the mouse moves out of striking range, the cat will turn its head away and return to the balanced resting state. He called this the "righting reflex." Magnus noted that in all the cats' movements, "the head leads and the body follows."

The work of Jones and Magnus can be combined to enable us to understand that through interfering with head balance *the startle pattern can disrupt the efficacy of our "righting reflexes," thereby becoming a habitual, "attitudinal" pattern*. This "attitude of startle" undermines the natural balanced resting state.

DOWNSHIFTING. *Downshifting* is a term coined by Dr. Leslie Hart to describe a fear situation that causes the brain to "disconnect" from itself. In these situations, the upper part of your brain, the cerebral cortex (the more evolutionarily advanced part of your brain that serves as the locus for intellect and rational thought), becomes disassociated from the lower and more primitive areas of your brain, which tend to take over in fear situations. As neck tensing, shallow breathing, and a modified startle pattern posture become habit, downshifting becomes the norm. Many individuals who are considered to be genetically unintelligent or in some way learning disabled are, rather, fundamentally brain competent but stuck in a downshift association pattern.

YOUR ATTITUDE TOWARD LEARNING AND LIFE. Habitual startle pattern disturbs the balanced resting state and locks in a "downshift" of our learning ability. It distorts perception, limits mental and physical flexibility, and often results in counterproductive habitual patterns of action, such as avoiding new learning experiences and making excuses for failure even before trying.

Perhaps you have noticed the way people's attitudes toward life can be locked into their bodies: the clenched jaw and aggressive gait of the chronically angry person; the stooped shoulders and cringing posture of the "wimp"; the raised eyebrows and permanent sneer of the snob. For most of us, our personal manifestations of the startle pattern are more complex and sophisticated than the caricatures we have just described. Nevertheless, if we fail to monitor ourselves, applying the power of our consciousness, it is all too easy to become stuck in fear-based, self-limiting, psycho-physical "I can't" patterns. How can we free ourselves from the effects of "habitual startle" and unleash our magnificent capacity to learn?

TRANSFORMING FEAR

RECOGNITION. As we emphasized in the previous chapter, change is predicated on awareness. As soon as you recognize the sources and manifestations of fear in your own life, they will immediately become more accessible to change.

ACKNOWLEDGMENT, UNDERSTANDING, AND ACCEPTANCE are powerful allies in transforming fear. Fear is a universal phenomenon. No one—not even Clint Eastwood or Margaret Thatcher—is immune. Some people spend their whole lives running from it. Some try to cover it up with a mask of arrogance or self-righteousness. Others wallow in it and are overwhelmed.

It takes real courage to acknowledge our fears. As we

deepen our self-understanding and acceptance, the energy of fear is transformed into enthusiasm and passion. Make fear your ally, sharpening your focus and honing your awareness. And remember, there's often nothing to fear but fear itself.

STUDY MODELS OF EXCELLENCE.   Observe babies, champions, and other high-performance learners, focusing specifically on how they handle situations that in others might produce startle pattern responses.

A classic example is the performance of Olympic diving champion Greg Louganis. In the penultimate dive of the gold medal competition, Louganis slipped and banged his head on the diving board. Most competitors would have quit at this point and allowed themselves to be taken to the hospital. Louganis, however, returned for his final dive, and after centering himself and visualizing the perfect dive, produced a perfect "10" to win the gold. The key to his success was his ability to open and expand his mind and body under the kind of stress that usually forces contraction. Champions like Louganis embody the phrase "Feel the fear and do it anyway."

Everything you've learned thus far in *Lessons from the Art of Juggling* is designed to help you transform fear into success, awakening your full learning potential by turning "I can'ts" into "I cans." As you model excellence, practice visualization, appreciate the nature of your brain's vast potential, and learn to love your mistakes, your confidence in your learning ability will grow. As your confidence builds, you will become more successful in juggling, learning, and life. As you become more successful, your confidence will grow further.

There's one more critical thing. We've been suggesting it throughout, but it's time to make it explicit.

If you strive for profound change, and ever-deepening levels of learning, you must take a mind/body approach. You must learn to access your capacity for relaxed concentration and mind/body coordination. You must learn to reattain your natural poise by freeing yourself from the legacy of startle.

POISE—YOUR NATURAL STATE

Watch a baby playing with a ball or a Masai tribesman dancing and you are moved by the upright, free, elegant quality of the movement. Study great performers like Fred Astaire, Ella Fitzgerald, Joe Montana, or Meryl Streep, and you will notice that they make it look easy. Observe a tiger stalking its prey, a flamingo taking flight, or a praying mantis nibbling on an insect and you'll witness an exceptional grace and perfect economy of movement.

This is poise. The right amount of energy in the right place at the right time. When applied in both stillness and movement, the outcome is mechanically efficient and aesthetically pleasing. People often assume that poise is something you either have or you don't. In one sense they are correct, in that *everyone* has it. If you have ever experienced a moment in life when things seemed to fall effortlessly into place, then you know what we mean.

If you have been practicing the juggling method introduced in *Lessons from the Art of Juggling*, you've probably discovered that the best results are achieved by using appropriate effort. If you are trying too hard, you tense up and everything seems to be happening too fast as the balls go flying in all directions. On the other hand, if you try to relax you may find that you don't have the clarity of focus to toss the balls accurately.

The art of learning involves discovering the right amount of effort for the task at hand. In many areas of life it is possible to get results by trying harder, but with some things trying harder does not work. You will not, for example, improve your golf swing, your posture, or your love life by trying harder. Greater effort can exacerbate faulty patterns of action. Doing the wrong thing with more intensity rarely improves the situation. Learning something new often requires us to unlearn something old.

Give up trying too hard, but never give up.

—Anonymous

The way abides in nonaction yet nothing is left undone.

—Lao-tzu

What is the secret of undoing old patterns of tension and stress? How can you get more result with less effort? Before we explain, read the following story of appropriate effort:

Once upon a time, a master juggler was called in to fix a problem with a giant organization's computer system. Engineers had been working around the clock to get the system back on line, to no avail. The juggler asked a few questions and then walked over to the central processing unit and tapped it three times. Instantly, the system was restored. The master submitted an invoice for $100,000. Even though the intervention had saved the company millions, the head of finance was aghast at the size of the bill. He asked the juggling master why he charged so much for work that took only a few seconds. The master replied, "I charged you $1 for tapping and $99,999 for knowing where to tap."

The secret of unlearning, of releasing the power of poise, begins with knowing where to tap. As we learned through our investigation of the startle pattern, interference with our natural poise begins with a pattern of tension that manifests first in the contraction of the neck muscles. This shortening of the neck disturbs the balance of the head in relation to the body. As the home of your brain and the primary locus of your balance, vision, and hearing, the importance of your head balance can hardly be overstated! Moreover, receptors in your cervical spine (i.e., your neck) are responsible for a significant amount of the kinaesthetic feedback that orients you in space. Your kinaesthetic sense serves as a bridge between mind and body, linking your inner and outer worlds.

Leaving aside abstract, theoretical Cartesian musings, how, in a practical, everyday sense, do you know that you exist? How do you know if you are relaxed or tense, aligned or imbalanced? That's right, your kinaesthetic sense tells you.

Reattaining poise begins with preventing the contraction of the neck muscles that causes unreliable kinaesthetic feedback and *the discoordination of the entire mind/body system.* But preventing this pattern of discoordination is easier said than undone!

If the startle pattern is such a deeply ingrained habit, how can you learn to undo it, or what can you do to unlearn it?

THE ALEXANDER TECHNIQUE AND
THE ART OF UNLEARNING

The most effective method we have discovered for un-learning this pattern of contraction was developed by F. Matthias Alexander.

Born in Tasmania in 1869, Alexander was a Shake-spearean actor specializing in one-man shows of tragedy and comedy. His promising career was interrupted by a tendency to lose his voice in the middle of perform-ances. Alexander consulted the leading doctors, speech therapists, and drama coaches of his day, carefully fol-lowing their advice. Nothing helped. The average per-son would have given up and tried another line of work.

Instead, Alexander resolved to overcome his problem on his own, reasoning that something he was doing with and to himself was causing the problem But how could he discover the specific cause?

Alexander realized that he must find a way to get objective feedback. He began to observe himself in spe-cially constructed mirrors. After many months of de-tailed and thorough observation, he noticed a pattern that emerged whenever he attempted to recite:

1. He contracted his neck muscles, thereby pulling back his head.
2. He depressed his larynx.
3. He gasped for breath.

As he observed further, he noted that this tension pattern (which Jones would later call a modified form of the startle pattern) was associated with a tendency to push out his chest, hollow his back, and tense all the major joint surfaces of his body.

Alexander's continued observation confirmed that this pattern was present in varying degrees every time he spoke. Noticing that this pattern of misuse began to manifest the moment he *thought* of reciting, Alexander realized that he had to unlearn this pattern, reeducating his mind and body as a whole system in order to change. He discovered that the key to doing this was to pause prior to action, inhibiting his habitual pattern of contraction, and then focus on specific "directions" he evolved to facilitate a lengthening and expansion of his stature. Alexander described these directions as follows: "Let the neck be free, to allow the head to go forward and up, to let the back lengthen and widen." Alexander, creating an Australian version of a Zen koan, emphasized that these directions were to be projected "all together, one after the other!"

Repeated practice of this new method produced astounding results: Alexander not only regained full control of his voice, he also recovered from a number of persistent health problems and became famous on the stage for the quality of his voice and general stage presence.

People began to flock to Alexander for lessons, among them a group of doctors who had an amateur theatrical company. The doctors began to send their patients with chronic problems to Alexander—people with stress ailments, breathing problems, back and neck pain. Alexander was able to assist them in a surprising number of instances by helping them to learn a new coordination of mind and body.

The doctors were so impressed by Alexander's work that in 1904 they sponsored his setting sail for London to share his work with the world scientific community.

He arrived in London and soon became known as the "protector of the London theater," giving lessons to top actresses and actors of the day.

Alexander also influenced many notable figures in other fields, including Professor Raymond Dart, Nobel Prize winners Sir Charles Sherrington and Nikolaas Tinbergen, Aldous Huxley, the Archbishop of Canterbury, and Professor John Dewey. Dewey wrote the introduction to three of Alexander's four books, proclaiming in one of these that Alexander gave him the means to translate his own ideals of progressive education into practical reality. In Dewey's words: "The Alexander technique bears the same relation to education as education does to life itself."

Before Alexander died in 1955 he trained a number of individuals to continue his work. For many years the technique has been taught at the Royal Academy of Dramatic Arts, the Royal Academy of Music, the Juilliard School, and other top academies for musicians, actors, and dancers. Indeed, the technique has been a trade secret for people in the performing arts, including luminaries such as Paul Newman, Mary Steenburgen, Sting, Paul McCartney, Sir Georg Solti, and John Cleese. In recent years, the technique has been applied by professional and Olympic athletes, the Israeli Air Force, corporate executives, professionals, and individuals in all walks of life.

Alexander's work is based on a keen level of self-observation that includes:

- Developing an increasing awareness of inappropriate effort in such everyday activities as sitting, bending, lifting, walking, driving, eating, talking, and juggling. (Are you stiffening your neck and pulling your head back, raising your shoulders, narrowing your back, or bracing your knees to throw the balls, pick up your toothbrush, talk on the telephone, or turn your steering wheel?)

• Attention to the natural flow of breathing, noticing any interruption of this natural flow (e.g., are you holding your breath when catching or throwing a ball, when picking up a pen to write or when meeting someone new?).

• Maintaining an easy, visual alertness, a comfortable integration of central and peripheral focus. (Does your focus get hard and narrow or diffuse and "spacey" as the balls approach the top of the box? Do you furrow your brow, squint your eyes, and clench your jaw when attempting to concentrate?)

Gertrude Stein's brother, Leo, described the Alexander technique as "the means for keeping your eye on the ball applied to life!"

Alexander's work is at the heart of our approach to learning. It often provides the missing link in the discovery of relaxed concentration and the transformation of "I can'ts" such as the notorious:

"I CAN'T JUGGLE; I CAN'T EVEN CATCH!" Over the years, we've worked with many students who complained that not only were they unable to juggle but also that they weren't even able to catch a ball. When we've asked these students to give us a demonstration of their inability, we observe a common pattern: as the student grabs the ball, he tenses his neck muscles, holds his breath, and as he releases the ball into the air, his whole body contracts and stiffens and, in many cases, he closes his eyes. As the ball drops, the student cries, "See? I told you I couldn't catch!"

In these cases, we begin by helping the student become aware of what he is doing to himself (i.e, going into a startle pattern at the very thought of juggling). Then, applying Alexander's principles, we guide the student to inhibit this fear-based reaction while breaking the task into its simplest components (i.e., just throw the ball to the top of the box without even thinking about catching it; focus instead on letting the neck be free, head forward and up, back to lengthen and widen). With a little patience and continuing attention to Alexander's "directions" for the integration of mind and body, the balls start to land in the students' hands. The results are inspiring. Typical comments include: "It's a miracle, it's the first time I ever caught a ball!" and "I was throwing two balls and all of a sudden the rhythm just happened!" After juggling three balls for the first time, a sixty-year-old student exulted, "I've just done the impossible!"

Part of our enthusiasm for the Alexander technique comes from Michael's experience of studying it for three months while doing no juggling whatsoever. In stopping his juggling for this period and focusing on poise, he released himself from restrictive, long-held startle pattern behavior habits. This resulted in a general improvement in his mind/body coordination, which manifested itself, when he returned to juggling, in immediate and dramatic breakthroughs! Tricks that had previously eluded him became easy, and he was able to make the breakthrough to five-ball juggling.

The best way to learn the Alexander technique is to have private lessons with a qualified teacher. Alexander teachers are trained to use their hands in an extraordinarily subtle and delicate way to guide you to free your neck and rediscover your natural alignment, in stillness and motion. In the meantime you can use this procedure, inspired by Alexander's work, to cultivate the state of relaxed concentration.

The Balanced Resting State

All you need to benefit from this procedure is a relatively quiet place, some carpeted floor space, a few paperback books, and fifteen to twenty minutes.

- Begin by placing the books on the floor. Stand approximately your body's length away from the books with your feet shoulder-width apart. Let your hands rest gently at your sides. Facing away from the books, look straight ahead with a soft, alert focus. Pause for a few moments.
- Think of allowing your neck to be free so that your head can go forward and up and your whole torso can lengthen and widen. Breathing freely, become aware of the contact of your feet on the floor and notice the distance from your feet to the top of your head. Keep your eyes open and alive, and listen to the sounds around you.
- Moving lightly and easily, sit on the floor. Supporting yourself with your hands behind you, place your feet on the floor in front of you with your knees bent. Continue breathing easily.
- Let your head drop forward a bit to ensure that you are not tightening your neck muscles and pulling your head back. Then, gently roll your spine along the floor so that your head rests on the books. The books should be positioned so that they support your head at the place where your neck ends and your

head begins. If your head is not well positioned, reach back with one hand and support your head while using the other hand to place the books in the proper position. Add or take books away until you find a height that encourages a gentle lengthening of your neck muscles. Your feet remain flat on the floor, with your knees pointing up to the ceiling and your hands resting on the floor or loosely folded on your chest. Allow the weight of your body to be fully supported by the floor.

• All you need to reap the benefit of this procedure is to rest in this position for fifteen to twenty minutes. As you rest, gravity will be lengthening your spine and realigning your torso. Keep your eyes open to avoid dozing off. You may wish to bring your attention to the flow of your breathing and to the gentle pulsation of your whole body. Be aware of the ground supporting your back, allowing your shoulders to rest as your back widens. Let your neck be free as your whole body lengthens and expands.

• After you have rested for fifteen to twenty minutes, get up slowly, being careful to avoid stiffening or shortening your body as you return to a standing position. In order to achieve a smooth transition, decide when you are going to move and then gently roll over onto your front, maintaining your new sense of integration and expansion. Ease your way into a crawling position, and then up onto one knee. With your head leading the movement upward, stand up.

• Pause for a few moments. Listen . . . eyes alive. Again, feel your feet on the floor, and notice the distance between your feet and the top of your head. You may be surprised to discover that the distance has expanded. As you move into the activities of your day, or into your juggling practice, think about not

doing anything that interferes with this expansion,
ease, and overall uplift.

For best results, practice the balanced resting state
at least twice a day. You can do it when you wake up
in the morning, when you come home from work, and
before retiring at night. The procedure is especially valuable when you feel overworked or stressed and before
or after juggling or any other exercise. Regular practice
will help you develop an upright, easy poise that encourages relaxed concentration in everything you do.

In addition to Alexander's work there are a number
of other disciplines designed to cultivate relaxed concentration. They include aikido, hatha yoga, the
Feldenkrais method, vipassana, and other forms of
meditation, Wilhelm Reich's orgonomy, Tim Gallwey's
approach to "inner" tennis, golf, and skiing, and tai chi
chuan. Each of these disciplines is worthy of further
study (see bibliography).

We particularly recommend the martial art of aikido
for those who seek to master the secrets of relaxed concentration. Aikido, literally translated as "the way of harmonious energy," is a Japanese martial art developed by
Morihei Ueshiba (1883–1969). Ueshiba achieved an en-
lightenment in which he realized his oneness with the
universe. He said, "The laws which define the structure
and dynamics of the universe must become part of our
awareness, for these are the same laws which determine
the structure and dynamics of the body. . . . The spirit
that moves an atom, waves the sea, lifts the flames of a
fire is also circulating in each human being."

Aikido is based on moving and breathing in harmony
with this essential spirit, known as ki, chi, prana, or "the
force." Ueshiba's insights of universal unity parallel
those of spiritual masters from many traditions, but his

particular genius was to develop a series of practical movements and partner exercises that, with regular and sincere practice, allow individuals to *embody* this perennial philosophy. One actually learns to be grounded but flexible like a willow tree, fluid like a wave, free like the wind, when facing would-be attackers and the stresses of everyday life. Indeed, we have both found that there is no better way to test one's freedom from the startle pattern than to stand facing a partner or partners who are preparing to hit you on the head with a big stick!

Of course, learning aikido takes many years of devoted practice. But to get you started we include the following mind/body meditation to add to your growing armamentarium of relaxed concentration skills.

Stand upright with your feet shoulder-width apart. Using your right hand, vigorously pound your left arm from the shoulder down to the fingertips. Imagine that you are chasing all the static, blocked energy out of your arm. Next, pound your right arm the same way. Then, in clockwise rotation, pound your stomach, and then, in classic Tarzan fashion, your chest. Now, with both hands, slap your left leg vigorously, starting at the top of your thighs. Imagine chasing stiffness and fatigue down your leg, through your knee, and out through your toes. Do the same thing with your right leg. Now, with both hands, pound your rear end and then, gently, your lower back. Next, massage your neck, scalp, forehead, and temples. Mush your cheeks around and massage your jaw. Good.

Now, without raising your shoulders, lift your arms up over your head and shake your arms for about ten seconds so that your whole body vibrates. Maintaining a lively, upright posture, let your hands fall to your sides while breathing out fully with an audible *ahhhhh*. Repeat this three times, allowing the *ahhhhhhh* to become richer and fuller each time. Now, feel your feet on the ground and, from a point just below your navel (your center of gravity), project your energy down so that you are rooted into the center of the earth. Breathe in through your nose, allowing the life force in the air to fill your entire being. As you exhale through your mouth, you let the breath wash away any remaining static energy. Maintaining your sense of connection with the earth, simultaneously project your awareness up from the point just below your navel. Imagine a stream of pure energy pouring up through your spine and out the top of your head, connecting you with the heavens. Your body stands as a bridge between heaven and earth. Stretch your arms out to the sides and then up over your head. Then, bring your hands together, left over right, at the point just below your navel. Let your mind rest at this point like a lotus blossom floating on a clear pond. As you approach your juggling and other life activities you can use this awareness of a still center within to enhance your capacity for relaxation-in-action.

With a free neck and a still center you will be poised to enter the juggling flow state. Of course, juggling itself is a tremendous tool for cultivating relaxed concentration. As you have probably noticed, it is hard to think of anything else while you are juggling. Juggling practice calms and focuses the mind while enlivening and balancing the body. The ambidextrous movement feels good and helps coordinate the two sides of the brain and body.

To progress in juggling, learning, and life, however, you must be able to work consciously on cultivating relaxed concentration. Perhaps, for example, you can maintain your poise, applying appropriate effort and focus with one or two balls, but what happens when you try three, four, or five? How about flaming clubs or chain saws? Maybe you are comfortable speaking to a group of 10 people, but what about a group of 100 or 1,000?

As we raise our level of difficulty in learning and life, the challenge to our poise grows greater. As you progress toward excellence in your chosen endeavors it becomes increasingly important to master the art of relaxed concentration. To further assist you in discovering the power of relaxed concentration, we created the following "Juggler's Meditation."

JUGGLER'S MEDITATION

I,
Juggler,
Stand between two spheres...
The expression
Of my Enlightened
Thoughts
Goes forward
And up
To the Sun.
The soles
And balls
Of my feet
Hug the loam of the Earth.

As I weave the dancing patterns of Infinity
Before me,
My entire body
Becomes:
More at ease;

More poised;
And more still
In motion:

The muscles of my feet, calves, and thighs
Balance the balled yin/yang
Of relaxed/alert;
My bellied center
Flows with the ki
Of Universal energy;
Stress flows from me;
My neck is free;
My head goes forward and up;
My back lengthens and widens;
My arms and hands are free
Playing the game of Spring
With Energy
And Gravity;

The sphere of my paraconscious senses
Extends to the infinite,
Dancing with the waves of the Cosmos
And open
As the Child.

I
Still
Play with Infinity
as I see
The balls
Individually
And in harmony,
As I
Feel the fleeting texture
In my receiving hands,
As I listen to the sounds

And silence
Of their landing and flying, flying and landing
As I sense my
Kinaesthesia moving them
Moving Me
(Do I play with them
Or they with me?)

My heart
Beats out a steady juggling rhythm
And jostles my blood-bundles
Through the opening and supple Pathways of my
heart's Life highways.
I breathe in
The molecules of stars
Exhaling rhythmically
A multi-billion cascade of
Atoms
As
I
Do.

As my limbs drop, rise and play with three,
My System
Juggles my quadrillion spheres the cells;
My quadrillion cells
Juggle their innumerable
Molecules,
They, Their innumerable innumerable atoms
And they in turn
Their microcosmos' more innumerable quarks—
the charms.
I
Am
Charmed.

Deeply
I am a juggler.
Deeply
I breathe out into the Universe
I have breathed
In:

Into the Universe.
Where suns
Juggle planets;
Where Galaxies
Juggle
Suns and their systems;
Where the Masked Juggler
Juggles
These ten-to-the-ten of the starry ten-to-the-ten
Constantly
Immaculately
Eternally.

I Atomic Child,
Charmed Child,
Star Child
Of the Universe
Juggle.

And
Am
Juggled.

GUIDELINES FOR THE ART OF RELAXED CONCENTRATION

Visualize yourself juggling with perfect poise. Check yourself again in the mirror or video screen while juggling. Observe the various parts of your body as you juggle—especially the head, neck, and shoulders— gently allowing each part to release in coordination with a general sense of expansion and upward flow through your entire being.

As you juggle, ask yourself: "What could be easier?" "What could be lighter?" "What could be more fluid?" And let your body answer.

Study the Alexander technique. To find a certified teacher, call the Society of Teachers of the Alexander Technique (STAT) at (44) 0171 351 0828.

Cultivate your ability to be poised under stress as you juggle multiple attackers by learning the martial art of aikido.

Make poise and relaxed concentration part of all your visualizations for all your learning activities.

1

. .
•   •

BECOMING THE
ULTIMATE COACH

One of the distinguishing features of the international
juggling community is the tradition of the free exchange
of tricks, patterns, tips, routines, and any other knowledge relating to the art. We welcome you to this gen-
erous tradition and offer this chapter as a means to
further enhance your own learning and juggling journey
while initiating that of others.

It's what you learn after you know it all that counts.
—*Coach John Wooden*

THE FALLACY OF THE "EXPERT"

Like the juggler who instructed Michael to "throw
these three balls into the air and don't let any of them
drop," many experts aren't very good teachers. Yet,

somehow the belief persists that expertise in a given area automatically qualifies the expert to be a teacher or manager. Our experience is that there is no intrinsic correlation between technical competence and teaching or management skill.

Experts are often poor teachers and managers because they have forgotten how to put themselves "into the mind" of a beginner. Frank Lloyd Wright once suggested that an expert is someone who has stopped thinking.

Of course, the ideal coach is one who combines expertise in a discipline with a practical understanding of the learning process. Even so, if you apply the principles in this chapter you may be surprised to discover that you can be an effective coach for anyone in just about anything.

WALK YOUR TALK

We believe that ultimately you are your own best coach. And that you earn the right to guide others by experiencing the process of growth and change for yourself. As your understanding of the "learning spiral" deepens it forms the spiritual sustenance with which you can begin nurturing others. It is essential to "walk your talk" when teaching, coaching, or leading others.

EDUCERE

The word *education* comes from the root *educere*, which means "to draw out" or "to lead forth." Unfortunately, many of us were schooled as though *educere* meant "to stuff in." If we are not careful, we can find ourselves applying this old model when guiding or coaching others.

In our experience the finest coaches and teachers create a context that brings out the best in their students. You can use the following elements to create a context of excellence and delight.

ELEMENTS OF EXCELLENCE IN COACHING

SET CLEAR GOALS. Guide your students to establish clear, multisensory images of their goals. Encourage them to write out and articulate their goals, and review them regularly. If you're coaching a team, we recommend that, with the help of your players, you put together a "mission statement" for your season.

GIVE ACCURATE FEEDBACK. Guide your students to discover accurate, objective information on the state of their current performance. In the words of coach Pat Riley of the New York Knicks and formerly of the world champion Los Angeles Lakers, "The job of a leader is to help people see reality."

FEED THE SUCCESS MECHANISM. Help your students discover the difference between current reality and the goal, creatively bridging the gap between them. For your students' "success mechanism" to function properly they need to compare the reality of current performance with the desired goal. Discover the right amount of creative tension for each student.

CREATE A FEAR-FREE ENVIRONMENT. Avoid using judgment or fear to manipulate. Rather, create conditions where fears are recognized, accepted, and transformed. Although fear can be used to get short-term results, in the long run it creates what John Dewey called "compensatory maladjustments."

CATCH YOUR STUDENTS DOING SOMETHING RIGHT!
When many of us were growing up, our parents, teachers, and coaches often tried to help us by pointing out everything we did wrong. It's all too easy to pass this approach on to the next generation. Although feedback on our mistakes is essential, it's also critical to know what we are doing that is working. Catch your students doing something right! Be careful, however, to avoid indiscriminately lavishing praise on students. Even though you mean well, this often backfires, creating a credibility gap. Give accurate, appreciative feedback.

GIVE ENCOURAGEMENT.
Create an air of inspiration and positive thinking in the learning environment. The heart of the word *encouragement* is courage. This quality of the heart is required to stretch ourselves beyond habit, embracing new learning.

BE PATIENT.
Remember the ebb and flow of the individual learning graph, with its stages of improvement, apparent setback, and plateaus. Seek to understand where each of your students is on their graph of progress and allow adequate time for the process to evolve.

NEVER USE HUMOR.
(Just kidding!) Use humor to reduce stress and fear. Transform anxiety with laughter. Friedrich Nietzsche, one of philosophy's great jugglers, said that humor is humankind's most divine quality. Keep a light perspective.

EXPECT SUCCESS. Maintain confidence in your students, based on your deep understanding of the innate capacities and design of the human brain. A growing body of research suggests that student performance is dramatically affected by teacher expectation.

In a study published in the *Journal of Applied Psychology* titled "Pygmalion Goes to Boot Camp: Expectancy, Leadership and Trainee Performance," army combat command instructors were told that a number of randomly selected trainees were gifted with superior leadership potential. At the completion of the fifteen-week course the researchers concluded that "trainees of whom instructors had been induced to expect better performance scored significantly higher on objective achievement tests, exhibited more positive attitudes, and perceived more positive leadership behavior." When the course instructors were debriefed and informed that the "superior" trainees had been selected at random, they refused to believe it!

Students sense your expectations of them not only through what you say but also, more powerfully, by the way you look at them, your facial expressions, and the tone and quality of your voice.

After every Olympics, gold medal winners are interviewed by the press. A reporter asks, "What's the secret of your success?" And champion after champion replies, "I couldn't have done it without my ——— (coach, mom, dad, uncle, husband, wife, friend), who always believed in me." Be the person whose belief in others changes their lives.

FREEDOM FROM EGO INVOLVEMENT. Fully committed to helping your students achieve their goals, you must avoid linking your own measurement of self-esteem to their performance. This balancing act tends to be particularly challenging and most important when coaching your own children.

ASK QUESTIONS. What happens in your mind when you are asked a question? Most people find that it causes them to . . . think! Use language that promotes a process of self-discovery for your students. In the spirit of *educere*, ask questions that lead your students to find things out for themselves. When more direct means are necessary, experiment with words such as *notice, observe, let, allow*—words that tend to inspire students to actively participate in the learning process.

PAY ATTENTION TO LEARNING STYLES. Different people choose to learn in different ways. Some people rely primarily on visual input. Others prefer auditory stimuli. Still others tend toward kinaesthetic experience. Some need an in-depth analysis of the task, while others just want the big picture. When working with individuals, seek to discover their preferred modes and communicate accordingly. Aim to encourage your students to develop their ability to learn in all modalities.

BE CREATIVE. Beyond different learning styles, each student is an individual and ultimately requires a unique approach. As Walter Carrington, one of the world's leading Alexander teachers suggests, "any way in is a way in." Keep searching for new and more effective ways to facilitate your students' progress.

ENCOURAGE EXCELLENCE. Challenge students appropriately, encouraging them to move beyond self-imposed boundaries to new levels of excellence. Sometimes, in reaction to the harshness of their own educational experiences, coaches can focus inordinately on trying to protect students' self-esteem, often through inaccurate positive feedback. Ultimately, this attitude undermines self-esteem and coddles mediocrity. Challenging your students to excel demonstrates your confidence in their ability to learn.

COACH "UNKNOWN" DISCIPLINES. One of the great ways to grow as a coach is to challenge yourself to help others learn subjects that you have not mastered yourself. (This is an essential skill for all managers.) In our longer residential management seminars we often devote a couple of afternoons to recreational activities. We coach our students in a variety of these activities in which we have developed some skill, such as juggling, running, swimming, and tennis. A client, Dave, once asked Michael, who has never played golf, for help with his game. Applying the principle of *educere*, Michael asked a few questions trying to ascertain Dave's goal and his current reality. Dave explained that he had a hitch in his swing that he couldn't seem to eliminate. As he watched the swing a few times, Michael noticed that Dave was tensing his right shoulder at the beginning of every backswing. Michael asked Dave to bring his awareness to his shoulder on the next few swings. Dave commented that he did not notice anything unusual. Michael realized that telling Dave about the likely cause of his hitch without guiding him to discover it himself would probably only make things worse. Dave needed clearer feedback, so Michael gently put his hand on Dave's shoulder and asked him to try the swing again. Dave exulted, "I'm raising my shoulder! That's the cause of this darn hitch." On his next shot Dave hit a perfect drive that actually hit the pin, and Michael retired from coaching golf!

Apply your powers of observation and knowledge of the learning process to facilitate learning in unfamiliar disciplines. A fringe benefit is that you will automatically begin to learn the more technical aspects of that discipline.

FACILITATE RELAXED CONCENTRATING.   Poise is often the missing link in a learning situation. Guide your students toward an integration of mind and body. As Michael did with Dave, guide your students to discover and release unnecessary tensions. Remember that most people do not know how to translate the command "Relax!" into physical reality. So instead, create an atmosphere that is conducive to relaxed concentration.

ACCESS "BEGINNER'S MIND."   Seek opportunities to learn from students and others more skilled than you to keep the learning process alive. Avoid the pitfalls of the "expert syndrome." Put yourself in unfamiliar, challenging situations where you become "as a child"; this will keep you free from the stifling arrogance and complacency of the know-it-all.

As George Leonard gracefully points out, "In the master's secret mirror, even at the moment of highest renown and accomplishment, there is an image of the newest student in class, eager for knowledge, willing to play the fool."

ASK YOUR STUDENTS TO TEACH.   William Faulkner wrote, "I don't know what I think until I've read what I've written." Frequently, we aren't aware of how much we have learned until we express it to someone else. Furthermore, teaching what we've learned forces us to integrate and incorporate our learning at a deeper level.

Encouraging your students to teach what they are learning accelerates their path to mastery.

ENCOURAGE PLAY. Play is the secret of accelerated learning. Invent games, access the imagination, use drama, make it fun!

Who learns more in a dialogue between a wise man and a fool?

LOVE YOUR STUDENTS. Love is the ultimate brain nourishment.

Coaching and teaching are undervalued in Western cultures. In the East, things are different. In Japan, for example, a teacher is called *sensei*. This title is one of great respect and honor. We pay lip service to the importance of education but underfund our schools and underpay our teachers. Teaching and coaching are often viewed as a dumping ground for individuals who can't really *do* anything worthwhile. The pernicious but prevalent assumption is that "Those who can, do. Those who can't, teach." This notion is one of our pet peeves. Tony provides our response in the following poem:

THOSE WHO CAN

"Those who can
Do:
Those who can't
Teach"

Sure, Sure, Sure,
Shaw.

Why not try telling that to:

Einstein;
Buddha;
Curie;
Christ;
Ueshiba;
Jefferson;
Leonardo;
Muhammad.

Those whose
Kant
Is "those who can't . . . "
Don't
Realize
That those who say
"Those who can't, Teach . . ."
Don't
Teach
and Don't
Do what it is most important
to Do.

Those who Can
Do
And Do
Teach.

GUIDELINES ON COACHING

• Coach a friend and then be coached by a friend while another friend monitors the process between the two of you. (If you follow the lessons of this chapter, you'll have plenty of friends with whom to practice.)

• Study models of excellence in coaching. Incorporate the skills of the best guides and teachers you have ever met. Learn what not to do from your worst teachers.

• Whenever you are at an impasse in your juggling, learning, or your life, ask yourself the question "What would my ideal coach say?"

PART 3

BEYOND INFINITY...

For those of you who have begun to "master infinity," the next three chapters take you "beyond infinity" into the realm of mega-multiple juggulation and the domain of the "Superbaby!"

The principles of Lessons from the Art of Juggling *will continue to apply throughout these advanced sections, as we hope they will apply throughout your life.*

- commitment to change
- relaxed concentration and poise
- self-coaching

EXPANDING YOUR KINAESPHERE

The level of freedom you have experimenting with new tricks will be determined by the effortlessness with which you can perform the three-ball cascade. One way to cultivate this effortlessness as well as to learn a very impressive advanced juggling trick is to practice with your eyes closed. By doing so, you develop much greater dependence on your kinaesthetic sense; you begin to develop a sense of the *kinaesphere*, the area of space around your body in which most of your juggling tricks will take place. This will help you with your other advanced tricks.

ADVANCED WARM-UPS

In addition to refining your three-ball cascade, there are a number of warm-up activities that will prepare you for advanced juggling.

1. Perhaps the most important warm-up is to simply play with the balls. Practice throwing them high, letting them bounce, catching a ball off a bounce, throwing it off various parts of your body: knees, arms, feet, head. Experiment with creative variations. These playful experiments with one, two, or three balls will form the basis of most of the tricks you will be learning in this chapter.

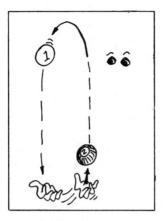

**TWO IN
ONE HAND**

2. Juggle two in one hand. Take two balls in one
   hand, pick a point just outside the top of the cor-
   ner of the box, throw the first ball to that point;
   when that ball reaches its apex, throw the second
   ball. You make little circles with your hand,
   throwing the ball *away* from the center of your
   body. After you throw and catch two balls with
   one hand, you will have completed your first two-
   ball juggulation.

   This two-in-one practice is an essential element
   in many advanced juggling tricks. It will also form
   the basis for four-ball juggling. Be sure to practice
   the two-in-one juggling with both hands equally.
   When you become comfortable throwing the ball
   in a circular pattern away from the center of your
   body, you can experiment throwing the ball *toward* your body.

3. Another warm-up exercise for advanced tricks is
   the over-under exercise. The first part of this exercise is called "a pair of braces." In this exercise,
   you take a ball with your *right hand* and, behind
   your back, throw it up over your *left shoulder* to
   the front so it lands in your left hand. Then

with your *left hand* behind your back, throw the ball over your *right shoulder*, letting it land in your right hand. See the braces? Go back and forth over alternate shoulders, letting the ball land in alternate hands until you are comfortable throwing the ball behind your back.

When you have mastered that, try the second part of the exercise. Take the ball in your right hand, throw it under your right *leg*, catching it in your left hand. Do this back and forth. You can then try four throws under each leg, then four throws over each *shoulder*. Repeat with two throws under each leg, two throws over each shoulder. Then one throw under each leg, one throw over each shoulder. Throw over the shoulder, catch behind the back. Then improvise from there.

Besides preparing you for tricks you will soon learn, this over-under exercise is also an excellent way to expand your kinaesphere. As you practice the over-under exercise you develop greater awareness of your whole body and the space that surrounds it.

ADVANCED TRICKS

(In learning these advanced tricks, it is especially useful to have one odd-colored ball.)

1. Shoot for the Moon: Start by juggling three balls in the basic cascade. When the odd-colored ball comes to your right hand, throw it up the middle, beyond the top of the box, pause for a moment while holding the other two, and let the high toss come down

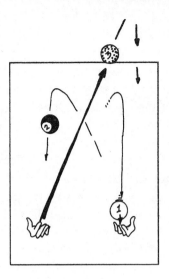

SHOOT THE MOON

in your left hand. You will have to throw the ball in your left hand up to the top of the box just before your high toss lands in your hand. Then continue your juggling cascade. When you get comfortable with the high toss, you can experiment with throwing the ball higher and higher, waiting for it to come down. Although it is a relatively easy trick, it will delight you and your audience.

Experiment with variations such as throwing the ball up high and doing a pirouette before letting it land in your opposite hand; try doing a somersault; a split; clapping your hands one, two, three, or four times; jumping up and down; and generally playing around while you wait for the ball to come down. Be sure to practice initiating this trick, and all your tricks, with each hand.

After you become comfortable throwing one ball "toward the moon," you can experiment throwing two of the balls out of your cascade into a high toss in succession (with any one of the variations previously mentioned). Then you can do the three-ball moon shot,

tossing all three balls beyond the top of the box in succession. Experiment by throwing them higher and
higher, pirouetting, somersaulting, or clapping as you
wait for them to return from orbit. These tricks are
simple but impressive.

2. Dropping the Balls: This is a trick you will in-
advertently do many times. It's worth practicing it consciously, both because it can be a fun trick to perform
and because it hones your reflexes so that when you *do*
drop, you can pick up the ball(s) and continue your
rhythm. In the basic one-ball drop, when your odd-
colored ball comes to the hand of your choice, throw
it up and let it drop, holding on to the other two, waiting for the odd ball to bounce back up to you. As it
bounces up, you release the ball in the hand with which
you are going to catch the dropped ball and incorporate
it back into your cascade. After you are comfortable
dropping one ball, drop two, then three. You can apply
many of the same variations you did while shooting for
the moon: pirouettes, handclaps, and so on.

3. The Reverse Infinity Series: The reverse infinity series provides a whole juggling show in itself. It is
a simple, elegant, and enjoyable trick to practice and
perform. When the odd-colored ball reaches the hand
of your choice, you will throw it over the top of your
juggling pattern. Practice throwing the same ball over
the top of your pattern every time it comes to the hand
of your choice. When you have become comfortable
throwing every third ball over the top, experiment
throwing every *other* ball that lands in the given hand
over the top of the pattern, and then *every* ball over
the top of the pattern. When you are comfortable doing
this from one side, try the same thing from the other

side. If you started throwing the balls over the top with your right hand, then practice the reverse cascade series starting with your left hand. Every time the odd-colored ball lands in your left hand, throw it over the top of the pattern. Start with every third throw, then every second ball that comes to your left hand will go over the top, and then every ball that comes to your left hand will go over the top. Once you are comfortable throwing every ball with your right hand over the top, and every ball with your left hand over the top, combine those two exercises. Whenever a ball lands in either your left or right hand, simply throw it over the top and you will be performing a reverse cascade. To make this exercise easier, imagine a large tube directly in front of you into which you are tossing every ball.

Although it seems very simple and at this point will probably be easy for you, this trick has a hypnotic effect on people. A nice variation on the reverse cascade series is to switch back and forth between the regular cascade and the reverse cascade five or six times. This creates a delightful "inside-out" visual effect.

4. The Fountain: The fountain begins in the same way as shoot for the moon. Take one ball from your left hand and throw it up the middle of the box approximately two feet over the top of the box. As that ball reaches its apex, take the two other balls and simultaneously toss them over the top of the box so that they cross in midair. While those two balls are crossing in midair and you are waiting for them to come down, your first toss will be plummeting to earth. Move a hand into the center, catch that ball, and flip it back up. Move your hands back out in time to catch the two balls that have crossed over. As those two balls land in your hands, you'll still have the one ball in the air that you tossed up the center. Incorporate it into your basic cascade, and you've just completed your first fountain.

Just as we did with the basic three-ball pattern, you will probably find it much easier to break this trick and perhaps some of the earlier tricks into their simplest elements:

- First throw the ball up the center.
- Then, cross the two over the top and let them drop while catching your central toss.
- Then, catch and retoss your central ball so that the crossing balls can land in your hands.

We recommend that you break all of these advanced tricks into simple elements, focusing, as you have throughout, on letting the balls drop into your hands, or not, as the case may be.

5. Body Bounces: There are as many body bounces as there are body parts! The most basic body bounce tricks are the arm bounce, the thigh bounce, and the head bounce. For the arm bounce, throw your odd ball so that it lands on any part of your arm, flick your arm against the ball to knock it back up toward the top of the box, and then reincorporate it into your juggling rhythm. The same holds true for the other body parts. For your thigh, drop the ball on your thigh, kick it up to the top of the box, and carry on from there. For the head bounce, we recommend that you do not use heavy balls. Other possible variations on this trick are to bounce the ball off your calf muscle, foot, wrist, elbow, and any other body part you choose. To make this trick easier, aim to release the ball as near as possible to the body part in question.

6. The Behind-the-Back Trick: The behind-the-back trick is a classic that audiences always request. It is a mark of a truly advanced juggler. The over and under warm-up provides the key to the behind-the-back trick (and to trick number seven, the under-the-leg trick). When the odd ball lands in your right hand, swing your right hand behind your back and throw the ball over your left shoulder so that it lands in your left hand. You'll probably find that it is best to begin by throwing the ball behind your back, over your shoulder, and letting it drop. At first don't even think about trying to catch the ball from behind your back. Instead, focus on making an easy throw behind your back, over your shoulder. With practice, you'll develop more control over that throw so that it begins to land near your opposite hand. As you become comfortable throwing the ball behind your back and over your shoulder and can catch it with your opposite hand, reincorporate it into your juggling rhythm. Be sure to practice the behind-the-back trick with each hand over the opposite shoulder. An *ultra*-advanced trick is to throw each of the

BEHIND THE BACK

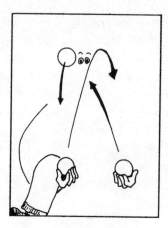

UNDER THE LEG

balls, one hand after the other, behind your back in a continuous rhythm.

7. The Under-the-Leg Trick: When your odd ball lands in your right hand, throw it under your right leg up toward the top of the box. At first you'll want to just focus on throwing the ball successfully under your leg—without thinking about catching it. As you become comfortable throwing the ball under the leg up to the top of the box, you can let it land in your opposite hand and incorporate it into your basic juggling pattern. Again, be sure to practice this trick under *both* legs. You can build from there, throwing every third ball under your leg until you reach the point where you can throw each ball under your leg with either hand.

8. The Famous Apple-Eating Trick: This is one of *the* classic advanced juggling tricks. When you tell people that you are a juggler, they will often ask, "Did you see that guy on TV who eats an apple while he juggles?" To which you can reply, "Yes, that seems really difficult" and then whip out your own *juggling*

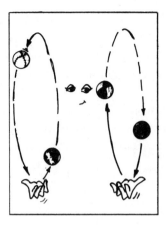

FOUR BALLS

apple and go to town! The secret to the famous apple-eating trick is to be able to juggle with two balls in one hand comfortably. The simplest way to do the trick is to take two balls and an apple (Golden Delicious are best because they are relatively soft) and juggle them in the cascade pattern, then break out of your cascade pattern into a two-ball juggle with one hand. Hold the apple in your other hand and take a bite out of it (quickly), then reincorporate it into your cascade.

When it reaches the hand from which you originally chomped it, take another bite, again juggling the two other balls in your opposite hand. (It takes a fair amount of control of the two balls in one hand to really enjoy your apple.) To make this trick effective, accelerate the pace at which you take bites of the apple, stuffing as much of it into your mouth as you possibly can and keep going until you have eaten just about the whole apple, at which point you slam it into your mouth, hold it there, raise your arms over your head, and take a bow with apple juice dripping down your chin, to the wild applause of your audience. It works every time!

9. Four Balls: The basic four-ball pattern involves juggling two balls in each hand at the same time:

- Practice the two-in-one exercise described in the basic warm-up.
- Juggle two balls in one hand away from the center of your body while looking straight ahead.

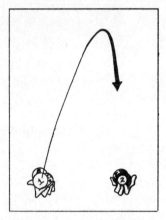

READY FOR FIVE BALLS

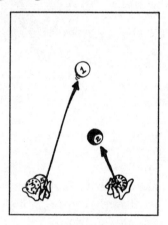

STARTING FIVE-BALL JUGGLING

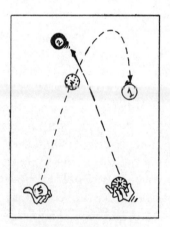

THROWING THE FOURTH BALL

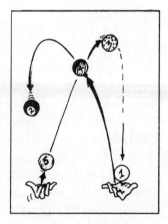

FIVE-BALL JUGGLING!

• When you are comfortable juggling two balls in each hand separately, you can combine them so that you are juggling two balls in each hand at the same time.

Voilà! You're juggling four balls! The secret is to move on from simultaneous tosses to staggered timing of your throws, thereby creating the illusion that the four balls are crossing over. Once you have this pattern going, you can begin to experiment with variations on this basic four-ball theme.

10. The Five-Ball Cascade: Juggling five balls involves the same pattern as three, only with two more balls. Begin with three balls in one hand, two balls in the other. At first practice simply throwing all five balls up to the top of the box in staggered timing (don't even think about catching them). You'll need to raise the top of your box about a foot or so for five balls. Let the balls drop just as you did in learning three balls. Keep practicing the release of the five balls as smoothly as you can and then begin experimenting with letting one ball land in your hand, letting two balls land in your hand, three, four, five, and so on.

JUGGLING THINGS OTHER THAN BALLS

Once you know how to juggle, you can juggle just about anything as long as you can lift it, toss it, and catch it. The most popular juggling objects besides balls are juggling clubs. Juggling clubs are marvelous tools of the juggler's art because they are highly visible, they create a pleasant audible rhythm, and they provide a lot of kinaesthetic satisfaction. Club juggling is a bit trickier than ball juggling because it requires that you spin the

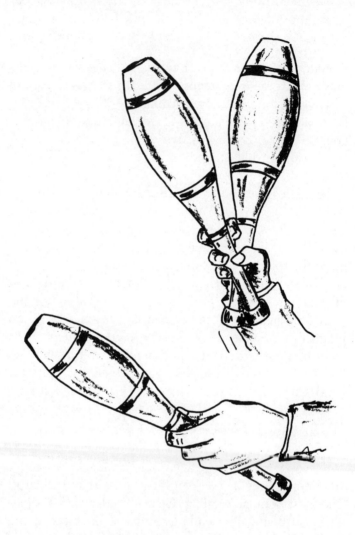

READY TO JUGGLE CLUBS

clubs as well as toss and catch them, but this is easy to
work out with a little practice. (Tip: Hold the club toward its center of gravity—this makes it much easier
to control.) Make, borrow, or purchase juggling clubs
and experiment for yourself.

Some other objects that are fun to juggle include
cigar boxes, scarves (easy!), eggs, objects of different
sizes and shapes, fruits, and basketballs. Use your imagination. One of the most amazing tricks we have ever
seen is the juggling of five Ping-Pong balls using the
mouth for throwing and catching.

Another example of imaginative object juggling
comes from an old juggling partner of ours who juggled
a chicken, a kitchen fork, and a turnip. This fellow purchased a rubber chicken from a novelty store and put
a baton down the chicken's throat to make it easier to
flip in the air. He juggled his chicken, kitchen fork, and
turnip while making chicken noises. After juggling this
motley collection for thirty seconds or so, he threw the
turnip high in the air, pointed his kitchen fork to the

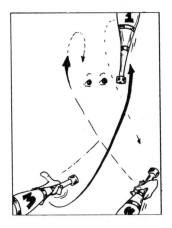

JUGGLING CLUBS

sky, and let the turnip land on the fork to enthusiastic applause. On one unforgettable occasion he tried this trick in front of an audience of 250,000 people at a Rolling Stones concert at the Knebworth Rock Festival—and missed! The turnip rolled off the stage (which was crafted to look like Mick Jagger's mouth). Waves of laughter rolled over the stage; then someone threw the turnip back on the stage, and, like a true juggler, he tried again. And this time it worked . . . to waves of tumultuous applause.

BUILDING YOUR OWN ROUTINE

As you begin learning tricks, you will start to think about how to combine them. Create a pattern—or patterns—in which one trick flows into another in a way that is kinaesthetically and visually enjoyable for you. Once you determine a basic sequence of tricks, practice it regularly until it becomes second nature.

Of course, sometimes you will want to practice by just fooling around and having your own "juggling jam session" with the various tricks. This kind of practice is fun and helps you discover new patterns. For performance purposes, however, you will want to have a "grooved" routine as a framework for your improvisations.

As you develop and groove your routine you may wish to begin performing. Before you unleash your juggling talents on the public, practice under challenging conditions: poor lighting, loud noises, a strong breeze. When you can easily adapt to a variety of distractions, you are ready for the bigtime. When you do perform, maintain your poise, keep contact with your audience, and above all, enjoy yourself.

By enjoying your juggling, (not worrying about mistakes) and following the above tips, you will be guaranteed a successful and entertaining performance. And, if you diligently apply the Juggling Metaphor Method in your practice, then your main challenge will be trying to make your tricks look difficult!

GUIDELINES FOR GOING BEYOND INFINITY

• Remember that progress to advanced levels in any discipline requires a willingness to explore new "trials" and to make new mistakes. Too often people get comfortable at a given level of attainment and lose the willingness to continue experimenting, learning, and growing. Nurture your love of learning by joyfully venturing into the unknown!

• When learning a new trick, throw the balls a bit higher to give yourself more time.

• Practice your three-ball pattern with your eyes closed.

• Improvise.

• When building your routine, note the *feel* of one trick as it flows into another and concentrate on finding the feeling that is most enjoyable to you.

• Think of all your tricks as *moving sculptures*, bringing the attitude of the artist to all your juggling.

• Your best tricks are usually created in moments of spontaneous joy emerging out of playful, childlike experimentation. Have fun!

9

. . .

INFINITE POSSIBILITIES

JUGGLING WITH COLLEAGUES, FRIENDS, FAMILY, AND LOVERS

One of the most satisfying results of mastering the basics of one-, two-, and three-ball juggling is that with just a few minor adjustments, you can juggle with a partner!

These advanced, more social techniques will not only improve your repertoire and skill but can also create and strengthen the bond between you and your partner in the context of learning and play. Your partner-juggling options are vast. In this chapter, we will introduce a few of the simplest and most enjoyable.

1. The Embrace: Stand side by side with your partner, facing the same direction. Put an arm loosely around each other, leaving one free arm each. Now the *two* of you are the equivalent of *one* juggler. Begin by tossing one ball back and forth, then go on to the two-ball pattern, following the same instructions

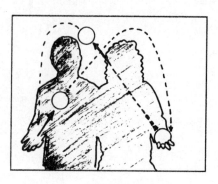

EMBRACE

as you would if you were juggling two balls on your own. The real fun begins when you juggle three. One of you will start with two balls, the other with one ball. The person with two balls throws one to the top of the box you have created between you. When it reaches its apex, the person with one ball throws it across, and you're on your way to juggling three balls using two hands and two bodies. Once you've got the cascade going, you can do most of the tricks mentioned in the last chapter or make up your own new tricks.

2. Front Stealing: Your partner stands opposite you juggling three balls in the basic cascade. Juggle a little bit higher and slower than usual. Watch the three-ball pattern carefully and pick out the odd ball. Say to yourself, "When the odd ball leaves my partner's right hand and comes up to the top of the box, I will put my right hand underneath it just as it reaches its apex." Practice stealing one ball out of your partner's cascade.

After you have the first ball landing easily in your hand, you can practice taking the first ball with one hand and the second ball with your other hand as it reaches its apex. When you have taken the first ball with one hand and the second ball with your other hand, you'll notice that the third ball, which your partner has just thrown up, is in the middle of the two balls you are holding. Treat your partner's last throw as your first toss, then continue juggling with all three balls.

You have just stolen the balls. Your partner will then steal them from you in the same manner, and you can go back and forth. The key to making this trick effective is that when you are the juggler, continue moving your hands as normal, as if the balls were not being taken. This creates a surprising and delightful visual effect.

3. Passing Routines: This passing routine is based on the same pattern that we followed when learning the reverse cascade series. Instead of throwing every third ball over the top, then every other ball over the

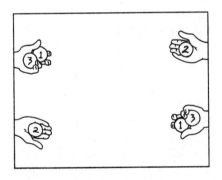

READY FOR PASSING

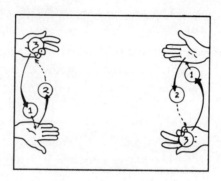

PASSING: STEP ONE

top, then every ball over the top, you are going to throw them across to your partner in the same rhythm.

Begin by facing your partner, each with two balls in your left hand and one in your right. Facing each other, you both raise your hands, lower them, and begin juggling at the same moment. When the single (odd) ball that was originally in your right hand lands in your left hand (it will be ready to become your fourth toss), you throw it across to your partner. Each time the original odd ball returns to your left hand, you throw it across to your partner again. (See illustration.)

Initially it helps to count out loud together, and to both shout "Throw!" at the right moment. If you throw the ball accurately and gently to your partner's hand and your partner throws similarly to your hand, you will not have to worry about catching. After you have succeeded in throwing to each other ten times, you can then switch to throwing *every other* ball across to your partner.

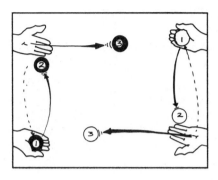

PASSING

When you have done that ten times, you can throw *every* ball across to your partner. The faster the rhythm becomes, the more important it is to focus on the throw. If you remain focused on the throws, the balls will keep landing in your hands.

GUIDELINES FOR JUGGLING WITH COLLEAGUES, FRIENDS, FAMILY, AND LOVERS

• Be sensitive to your partner's style, and adapt your juggling to fit your partner.
• Always make your partner look good. Play to your partner's strengths. Bring out his or her best.
• When throwing a ball to your partner in a passing routine, toss the ball in a gentle arc so it lands softly in your partner's hand. Never throw the ball *at* your partner, always *to* your partner.

• Focus on your timing. The most critical aspect of team juggling is the synchronization of movement and thought. Breathe with your partner's rhythm. Think of yourselves as a *whole unit*, as one integrated phenomenon.

• Apply these principles to all your relationships at home and at work.

10

· ·
·

SUPERBABY:

THE POWER OF PLAY

*In terms of game theory, we might say
the universe is so constituted as to
maximize the play.*

—GEORGE LEONARD

In our corporate seminars on creativity, learning, and
leadership, we usually ask our students to dress casu-
ally. Nevertheless, they often arrive with gray suits,
tight collars, and serious faces. They are usually stressed
out from the intense pressures of their jobs and am-
bivalent, if not downright hostile, about having to take
time away from the workplace. As we introduce the
program, involving them in practical exercises and re-
search-based, analytical justifications for the process,
they start to "buy in." At this point, we whip out the
balls and begin their first lesson in the art of juggling.

Consistently, something remarkable happens: jackets
and ties are removed, collars are loosened. Smiles,
laughter, and silly jokes fill the room. Executive grown-

ups become mischievous youngsters. Their faces relax and eyes open wider as they discover the power of humanity's most effective learning mode: play.

Play! An exclamation. A temptation. An exhortation. An interaction. A Shakespearean dream. An invitation.

Plato said, "Life must be lived as play. . . ." The ancient Greeks knew that play was the secret of learning. Their words for play (*paida*) and education (*paideia*) are slight variations on the same theme.

Play is the way all animals and children learn. It is a powerful catalyst for the development of all mental and physical skills. *Lessons from the Art of Juggling* is essentially a book about unleashing your full learning ability through the power of play. And to relearn the art of play, it's best to start by modeling the masters.

In every real man a child is hidden that wants to play.

—*Nietzsche*

OOOH! LOOK AT THE BABY!

Play and work are not separate for the baby. A baby's "job" is to explore the universe, so for the baby, work equals play. Watch a baby learning to walk.

The process consists of innumerable experimental attempts toward the goal of standing upright and walking on two feet. The baby will spend hour after hour crawling, nearly getting upright, falling, exploring, crawling, tottering, falling, while laughing at both the successes and the failures. (Can you imagine if after falling down a few times, the baby said, "Forget it! I quit! I obviously have no natural talent for walking!")

While learning to walk, the baby explores everything in its path: the taste and feel of the carpet, the tensile strength and smell of a piece of paper or Mommy's hair, the sound of a bottle banging against the crib wall. Like a little Isaac Newton, the baby delights in discovering all the synaesthetic delights of its universe.

To myself I seem . . . like a boy playing on the seashore . . . diverting himself and then finding a smoother pebble or a prettier shell than ordinary, while the greater ocean of truth lay all undiscovered before me.

—*Isaac Newton*

Similarly, in learning to talk, the baby will play . . . with sounds, words, rhythms, oral "feelings," volumes, pitches, and tones, constantly assessing the effects of the sounds it produces on Mommy, Daddy, brother, sister, dog, or cat.

Young children display similar playing skills in learning almost anything. Engaging their synaesthetic visualization, they imagine themselves as different beings or objects. This visualization and creative imagination often lead children to astounding awarenesses, which are frequently unappreciated by the more prosaic adults around them.

For example, one day, when Tony was riding the London subway, he was sitting just behind a five-year-old girl and her mother. The train was accelerating well beyond the normal speed for underground trains, and the little girl, becoming excited, exclaimed to her mother, "Mummy, wouldn't it be amazing if this train could keep going faster, until it was going so fast it could take us into tomorrow? We could then go home and tell Daddy what was going to happen in the future!" The mother responded, "Don't ever say such a stupid thing again."

In this case, the child was displaying extraordinary insight, playing with ideas in a way identical to Einstein's musings on the theory of relativity. Einstein imagined himself traveling out into the universe on an ever-accelerating sunbeam . . . and discovered tomorrow. And Einstein attributed his special insights into the universe to a willingness to explore questions of time and space through the eyes of a child.

WHO CAN LEARN FASTER, YOU OR A BABY?

Most adults would answer "Babies are better, faster learners." However, we believe it is possible for you, the adult learner, to learn even faster than a baby—to become a *superbaby*. You can learn faster than a baby if you are willing to combine a babylike playfulness with your adult cognitive skills and resources.

Take language learning, for example. Most people believe that a baby will learn languages far more rapidly than a seventy-year-old adult. Actually, the seventy-year-old can learn languages faster than the baby, if that adult learns *as a baby*.

Traditional language learning programs were based on an analytical approach. Students memorized verb conjugations and vocabulary words—it didn't work very well. Today the most effective language learning programs involve their students in a total experience.

For example, in a Spanish class we visited, students were dressed in sombreros and serapes. The walls were covered with colorful posters of Spain, Mexico, and other Spanish-speaking countries. Spanish music was playing in the background. The students were engaged in acting out a scene using only Spanish. When a mistake was made, the teacher simply repeated the correct word, phrase, or pronunciation, which the student then repeated. Emphasis was placed on expressive gesture and body language. The teacher was regularly "catching her students doing something right." The room was filled with animation and laughter. The students were learning—fast.

This joyful, brain-friendly approach to learning is much more effective. Our brains are designed to expand upon the baby's inherent and extraordinary abilities. We maintain that the healthy and natural state of the adult is that of the superbaby.

When they see us juggle, people sometimes ask whether we grew up in circus families, or were the children of professional jugglers. The assumption underlying this question is that one can only acquire such a skill during childhood. This assumption is almost right: One *can* only master such a skill by approaching it with the openness and enthusiasm of a child. It is the *method of a child* that makes the learning possible.

What then are the secrets of the child's method, the essential ingredients for actualizing our superbaby potential?

We are all infant prodigies.

—*Thomas Mann*

THE VITAL ELEMENTS OF PLAY

CURIOSITY: From birth, and some would argue, even before, the baby's every sense is involved in exploring the world. The first years of life are characterized by a seemingly unquenchable thirst for knowledge.

As soon as language is learned, children start asking questions: Why? Where? Who? When? What? and How? The answers provide new data that form the basis for even more questions.

A bright child can take the most educated adult to the boundaries of knowledge with a few simple questions. For example, in an imaginary conversation with Einstein, a child asked:

"Uncle Albert, what's a rainbow?"

"It is white light being broken down into its different colors by the curvature of a raindrop."

"But Uncle Albert, what's light?"

"It's either little bundles of energy or wave forms."

"But Uncle Albert, what's energy?"

"Good question!"

Asking incisive questions and reaching beyond the answers with more questions is essential to being a superbaby.

SYNAESTHESIA: Synaesthesia, the blending of the senses, has been a hallmark of genius throughout history. Albert Einstein, Nikola Tesla, Gustave Flaubert, Frank Lloyd Wright, Isadora Duncan, Henry Moore, Auguste Rodin, and many other greats cultivated this gift.

Babies naturally use this multisensory capacity, where color is equated with sound, rhythm with shape, taste with touch, and sight with feeling. Because synaesthetic observations can seem bizarre ("Oh, Mommy, listen to that big red flower!"), these abilities tend to be restricted ("That's silly, flowers don't make any noise)."

You can improve your memory, creativity, and enjoyment of the learning process by cultivating synaesthesia. Experiment, for example, by describing the texture, sound, and color of a perfect three-ball cascade.

ENJOYMENT, OPENNESS, AND WONDER: Notice the light in the baby's eyes, the easy laughter and frequent smiles that accompany the baby's explorations. For the baby, delight of discovery is its own reward. Babies have an obvious advantage when it comes to viewing the world without preconception or prejudice. Their open awareness creates total receptivity to new information.

In a classic Zen parable, a master invites his student for tea. The master pours the tea. The student's cup is filled, but the master continues to pour. As the cup overflows, the student cries out, "But master, my cup is full, it's overflowing." The master replies, "So it is with your mind. If you are to receive my teaching, you must first empty your cup."

Empty your cup. Open your mind. Poet John Keats called this ability "a receptivity to all things" and emphasized that it was a key characteristic of genius.

Psychiatrist Erich Fromm emphasizes that creative learning "requires the capacity to be puzzled. Children still have the capacity to be puzzled. But once they are through the process of education, most people lose the capacity of wondering, of

*being surprised. They feel they ought to know everything,
and hence that it is a sign of ignorance to be surprised or
puzzled by anything."*

SERIOUSNESS/INTENTION: What is often dismissed as
"child's play" is truly a very serious activity. Even
though the baby is often laughing while learning, careful observation reveals the child is dedicated, intent,
and fundamentally serious about the task at hand.
Adults often comment that children have short attention spans; what that really means is that children do
not necessarily attend to adult priorities. When children
are engaged in pursuing their own agendas, their power
of attention is prodigious.

In many of the organizations we visit, people tell us
that they are afraid to be playful for fear of being dismissed as not serious. They point out that a tense and
miserable demeanor gives others the impression that
hard work is being done. Instead, work smart. Over-
seriousness is a warning sign for mediocrity and bureau-
cratic thinking. People who are seriously committed to
mastery and high performance are secure enough to
lighten up. Create an environment where it's safe to be
serious about the importance of play.

---

*We are most nearly ourselves when we achieve the serious-
ness of the child at play. . . .*

—*Heraclitus*

PASSION AND INVOLVEMENT: If a baby toddles into a
room full of adults, everyone turns and says something

like: "Ooohh, look, a baby!" The baby's passion, involvement, and aliveness make it naturally charismatic.

Babies are passionate in pursuing their desires. They don't hedge their bets. As any parent will tell you, when a baby wants something it goes all out to get it! Superbabies are the same. In a classic study, chess experts were compared with grandmasters. The researchers were unable to find any differences in IQ or memory ability between the two groups. The only factor that distinguished the grandmasters was that they spent more time playing because they were more passionate about the game.

As George Bernard Shaw suggested, "This is the true joy in life. The being used for a purpose, recognized by yourself as a mighty one; the being thoroughly worn out before you are thrown on the scrap heap; the being a force of nature instead of a feverish little clod of ailments and grievances complaining that the world will not devote itself to making you happy."

Find healthy passion and nurture it. Be a force of nature. Play with all your heart.

REPETITION/PRACTICE: Babies are notorious for repeating things over and over again. Repetition gives the trial and error process time to work. Babies experiment, test, find out what works and what does not. By repeating a new word or action for days on end, the baby incorporates its new learning, "grooving" new neural pathways.

Superbabies understand the importance of the famous one-liner of the young tourist who lost his way in New York City. He stopped a police officer and asked: "How do I get to Carnegie Hall?" The officer replied, "Practice, my boy, practice."

RELAXED CONCENTRATION: Put your hand on a baby's back and you can feel the energy flowing through its entire being; you can sense the "wholeness." Babies move without unnecessary tension—spines lengthening as they crawl, sit, or stand. Babies' "relaxation-in-action" gives them extraordinary strength and resilience and explains why they rarely injure themselves when falling. Poise is our birthright. As we unlearn unnecessary patterns of tension, it reemerges and with it a growing ability to play with enthusiasm and joy.

PRACTICE UNCONDITIONAL SELF-ACCEPTANCE: Many of us give ourselves a hard time when we try to learn something new. We internalize the views of our worst critics and berate ourselves ruthlessly for the slightest mistake. If we treated our children the way we treat ourselves, they would never learn to walk or talk. Can you imagine saying to a two-year-old, "Look you little cretin, if you can't pronounce it properly then just shut up!" or "Stop falling down, spastic. Get up and walk straight or don't walk at all."

Scientists have begun to demonstrate that infants need love, in the form of cuddling and soothing encouragement, as a fundamental requirement for healthy brain development. Love is the greatest fuel for the process of learning. If you watch a baby learning to walk or talk, chances are your heart opens and you naturally offer your love.

When you were a baby, your parents were responsible for nurturing your learning process with unconditional love. They did the best job they could, given the limitations of their own upbringing. Now that you are a grown-up, you are responsible for nurturing your own learning process. Begin by giving yourself the love and encouragement you would give to a baby. With self-acceptance as your point of departure, seek an accurate awareness of your current reality. Set ambitious goals and enjoy the tension between your goals and reality. Bridge the gap with joyful, serious play.

THE EVOLUTION OF THE HUMAN BRAIN AS A LEARNING MECHANISM

Why is it that humans are so naturally gifted as learners? The answer can be found in the millions of years evolution has spent developing the most advanced biocomputer on the planet—your brain. It's so powerful that the most sophisticated computers pale by comparison. The survival of the spearhead of evolution, the human species, is predicated on one major distinguishing characteristic: flexibility.

The human child has the longest childhood of any creature. As a species we are able to spend unusually long periods of time with our children. All of this allows an unlimited number of behavioral options to be built into the developing brain. Nature's gift for exploring our options and realizing our potential is the most delightful, serious, and important of all human activities: PLAY!

In his groundbreaking studies of "self-actualizing" individuals Abraham Maslow observed that these extraordinary people possessed a quality he termed "second naïveté." If you study older people who have maintained their passion for life, you will find a sense of wonder, curiosity, irreverence, and involvement, just like babies! The Bible says, "Lest ye become as little children, ye shall not enter the Kingdom of Heaven." If you are willing to rediscover the openness, freedom,

and the wisdom of play. Juggle, and awaken the inner rhythm that links you to all creation. Whatever you have always wanted to learn, your greatest dream, your wildest fantasy, begin it now! Commit yourself and your success is inevitable.

Welcome to the growing family of universal jugglers! This poem is for you.

THE UNIVERSAL JUGGLERS: SOUND, FORCE, SPACE-TIME, ENERGY —THE GREAT CHILDREN OF THE COSMOS

The Universal Jugglers
The Great Children.
Infinite Gambolling!
Sound cascades, rolls and spreads, rises and falls,
*   breaks, blends, molds, enfolds, jumps, leaps, laughs.*
Force heaves, drives, tunnels, pierces, shakes, lifts,
*   tugs, blows, throws,*
drops, shrugs, sucks, whirls, stretches, hones, breaks,
*   combines, burns, laughs.*
Space-Time spreads, drifts, fades compresses, thins,
*   rolls, wafts, enfolds.*
Energy changes, shuffles, juggles, heats, beams,
*   heaves, radiates, explodes.*

Their Toys! Their Fields!
Limitless limbs to juggle, drop, rise, kick, hit, and
*   play!*
Jewel clusters to giggle over, spin, rotate; fireballs to
*   form,*
condense rocks around, paint with gamma's brush,
*   freeze,*

explode; ball as sun, planet, molecule, or atom to
    dribble, carry,
bowl, throw, kick, or spin. All to hurl, skip, swing,
    rollick, clown, play pranks on, laugh, dally, romp
    through:
X-ray gardens, gamma greenness, ultra, infra
    realities; Great Wastes,
Galactic clouds to peep from blind-man's bluff in
    Rorschach horses to mount and ride.

Around and around and through our straight, circled,
    speed-yoked universe!
Shooting for the moon, riding on flame-tailed ice balls,
looking to things looming from Titan's only blue
    horizon, seeing filigree
of star-dust spectra tantalizing to us, laughing at:
    winged helmet;
slit symbolized; sphere crossed; war arrowed prick
    head; bolt;
Kronos; his spawner; trident; infernal god; and dust;
    our spinning stones;
kicking about blue stars full circling red is heat to
    blue is cold,
tampering with Cluster, Nebula, shackled suns,
    tandem
travelers, and Supergiant, absorbing all colors, seeing
    Monster
exploded into Crab, Light dust-belted, Supernova
    shattered, and the
Cosmos Red shift and Blue shifting us into cube into
    cube into cube
into nothingness is Everything.

Infinitely Energetic, Boundless, Unchained!

all days and the seventh the same into One. Free!
   Superbabies playing,
playing through us, lasers, heat, fire, juggle, bounce,
   penetrate, mold
form, all these are Theirs, Eternity Infinite Dark,
   Light, Create, Destroy,
Never grow old!

Change consumes to Changed: movement uniform,
   speed constant, noise none;
They echo in Single Tones.

MILESTONES TO INFINITY: THE MASTER JUGGLER GRID

Many of our students have asked for a system for measuring their juggling progress. In response, we have created the master juggler grid. Formal ranking grids are used in a wide range of pursuits, from piano playing to chess and the martial arts. Our grid is modeled on the ranking system used in the Japanese art of aikido, of which we are both students. Although we trust that you will find this grid useful in measuring your juggling progress, our main wish is that your application of the principles of *Lessons from the Art of Juggling* will provide you with immeasurable joy and richness in all your learning and throughout your life.

10th level—Juggling one ball ten times back and forth from hand to hand.

9th level—Throwing two balls to the appropriate points at the top of the box in staggered timing and letting them drop. Throwing two and catching one. Throwing two and catching both—a two-ball juggulation.

8th level—Ten juggulations with two balls.

7th level—Throwing three balls to the appropriate
points at the top of the box and letting them all
drop. Throwing three and catching one. Throwing
three and catching two. Throwing three and catching three—your first three-ball juggulation!

6th level—Three complete, continuous juggulations.

5th level—Ten complete, continuous juggulations.
Successful completion of one shoot for the moon.
One one-hand juggulation with each hand individ-
ually.

4th level—Thirty-three and one-third complete, continuous juggulations (100 throws). One ball over
the top from either side, three times continuously.
Five one-hand juggulations with two balls (10
throws) with each hand individually.

3rd level—One hundred complete, continuous juggulations (300 throws). One complete, continuous
reverse infinity series. Three fountains in a continuous series of juggulations. Twenty one-hand juggulations with two balls (40 throws) with each
hand individually. Over/under exercise with one
ball, ten times.

2nd level—Three hundred thirty three and one third
complete, continuous juggulations (1,000 throws).
The behind-the-back trick, in the flow of a juggulation, with either hand. One hundred one-hand
juggulations with two balls (200 throws) with each
hand individually. Body-bounce trick, in the flow
of a juggulation, on the body part of your choice.
Throwing a ball over your shoulder, catching behind your back—ten times on each side.

1st level—All of the previous requirements, with a
demonstrable improvement in the quality of poise,
rhythm, and flow. The behind-the-back trick, in
the flow of a juggulation, with both hands, con-

secutively. The over-the-shoulder trick, in the flow, with both hands, consecutively. Four-ball flash (one complete juggulation). One-minute juggling routine incorporating at least four different tricks, including one created by the juggler.

Black Belt—All of the previous requirements, with a demonstrable improvement in the qualities of poise, rhythm, and flow. Four-ball juggling for thirty seconds, continuously (approximately twenty-five juggulations). Five-ball flash (one complete juggulation). Two-minute, three-ball routine incorporating at least eight different tricks, including three created by the juggler.

2nd degree Black Belt—All of the previous requirements, with a demonstrable improvement in the qualities of poise, rhythm, and flow. Four-ball juggling routine for one minute, incorporating three different tricks. Five-ball juggling for three juggulations, continuously. Three balls in one hand, two juggulations.

3rd degree Black Belt—All of the previous requirements, with a demonstrable improvement in the qualities of poise, rhythm, and flow. Four-ball juggling routine for two minutes, incorporating six different tricks. Five-ball juggling for twenty seconds, continuously. Six-ball flash (one juggulation). Smooth, seven-ball drop!

GLOSSARY

Aikido—Literally "the way of harmonious energy." A martial art based on nonviolence.

Alexander Technique–A method for unlearning the startle pattern and accessing the state of relaxed concentration.

Cascade—The basic three-ball juggling pattern. It looks like a figure eight on its side.

Flow State—A state of relaxed concentration where complex tasks seem simple.

Juggulation—Throwing and catching three balls in sequence.

Mind Maps®—A method for juggling with thoughts that improves creativity, memory, and learning ability.

Quality—The result of a total commitment to continuous learning.

Shower—Juggling in a circle, with the balls passed hand to hand at the bottom of the pattern.

Startle Pattern—A fear state characterized by a tense neck and retroflexion of the head.

Superbaby—An adult learner with the openness, curiosity, and commitment of a child.

BIBLIOGRAPHY

Alexander, F. M. *The Use of the Self.* London: Methuen, 1932. Reprinted by Victor Gollancz, London, 1985. The author's fascinating account of his discovery of the Alexander technique. Essential reading for anyone wishing to learn the art of relaxed concentration.

Bennis, Warren. *On Becoming a Leader.* New York: Addison-Wesley Publishing Co. Inc., 1989. Bennis's profile of twenty-eight leaders, including James Burke, Betty Friedan, and Norman Lear, shows that the ability to bounce back after dropping the balls is a key to success.

Buzan, Tony. *The Mind Map Book: Radiant Thinking.* London: BBC Books, 1993. Buzan's masterpiece, the ultimate guide to mind mapping.

———. *Use Your Head.* London: BBC Books, 1989. Buzan's classic work established him as the father of "whole-brain" education. An invaluable guide for anyone interested in learning how to learn.

———. *Use Your Memory.* Revised and updated. London: BBC Books, 1989. The best of the "how-to" memory books. Buzan deals with the subject comprehensively; his techniques are easy to learn and immediately applicable.

Covey, Stephen. *The 7 Habits of Highly Effective People.* New York: Simon & Schuster, Inc., 1989. Systematized common sense.

Dobson, Terry and Miller, Victor. *Aikido in Everyday Life: Giving in to Get Your Way.* Berkeley, CA: North Atlantic Books, 1993. This book demonstrates a variety of creative strategies, based on the metaphor of aikido, for dealing with conflict in everyday life.

Fincher, Jack. *Lefties: The Origin and Consequences of Being Left-Handed.* New York: Putnam, 1977. An amusing and well-researched overview of the relationship between hand and brain.

Fuller, Buckminster. *Critical Path.* New York: St. Martin's Press, 1981. Fuller emphasizes that the vast potential of the brain is released through the process of trial and error.

Gallwey, W. Timothy. *The Inner Game of Tennis.* London: Pan Books, 1986. Accessible, athletic Zen.

Gelb, Michael J. *Body Learning: An Introduction to the Alexander Technique.* Revised and updated edition. London: Aurum Press, 1994. *Publishers Weekly* called this the most lucid book on the subject.

————. *Present Yourself: The Simple Way to Give Powerful and Effective Presentations.* London: Aurum Press, 1988. An *Elements of Style* for creative speakers.

————. *The New Mind Map.* Washington, DC, 1991 (illustrated by Nusa Maal Gelb). A road map for your mind.

Hart, Leslie. *How the Brain Works.* New York: Basic Books, 1975. Leslie Hart provides a fascinating look at the working of the human brain, emphasizing particularly its active, pattern-seeking nature.

Heckler, Richard Strozzi. *Aikido and the New Warrior.* Berkeley, CA: North Atlantic Books, 1985. Includes Terry Dobson's powerful essay on conflict resolution, "A Kind Word Turneth Away Wrath."

Herrigel, Eugene. *Zen in the Art of Archery.* Harmondsworth: Penguin, 1993. The original Zen application book, it offers penetrating insights into attaining excellence in any discipline.

Hoffman, Edward. *The Right to Be Human: A Biography of Abraham Maslow.* Los Angeles, CA: Jeremy P. Tarcher, Inc., 1988. A charming biography of the father of humanistic psychology and human-centered management.

Jones, Frank Pierce. *Body Awareness in Action: A Study of the Alexander Technique.* New York: Schocken Books, 1976. This excellent book includes an extensive discussion of Jones's groundbreaking scientific study of the Alexander technique, including his work on the startle pattern.

Leonard, George. *The Silent Pulse.* Harmondsworth: Arkana, 1992. Leonard juggles music, physics, philosophy, mathematics, and sports in his quest for the "perfect rhythm."

————. *Mastery.* New York: Dutton, 1991. An eloquent invitation to a lifetime of learning.

Samuels, M. and Samuels, N. *Seeing With the Mind's Eye.* New York: Random House, 1976. This comprehensive work provides fascinating information on the history and uses of visualization.

Saotome, Mitsugi, *Aikido and the Harmony of Nature.* Boston: Shambhala, 1993. Saotome provides an inspiring model of relaxed concentration.

Selye, Hans. *The Stress of Life.* New York: McGraw-Hill, 1978. The original work on stress, which introduced the notion of "fight or flight."

Senge, Peter M. *The Fifth Discipline: The Art & Practice of the Learning Organization.* London: Century Business Books, 1993. An organizational guide to learning how to learn.

Summers, Kit. *Juggling with Finesse.* San Diego: Finesse Press, 1987. A compendium of jugglerian models of excellence.

Tzu, Lao. *Tao Te Ching.* Harmondsworth: Arkana, 1989. The bible of nondoing and unlearning.

Von Oech, Roger, *A Whack on the Side of the Head.* Revised Edition. London: Thorsons, 1990. Von Oech celebrates the power of play to unleash the creative process.

Walton, Mary. *The Deming Management Method.* London: Mercury Business Books, 1989. A quality book about quality.

THE JUGGLING METAPHOR METHOD
—(SHORT VERSION)

1. Take one ball and toss it back and forth, from hand to hand, in a gentle arc just above your head. Good!
2. Take two balls, one in each hand. Toss the ball in your right hand just as you did with one ball. When it reaches its high point, toss the ball in your left hand in exactly the same manner. Focus on smooth, easy throws, and let both balls drop.
3. Same as step 2, only this time catch the first toss. Let the second one drop.
4. Same as step 2, only this time catch them both!
5. Great! Now you are ready to try three balls. Take two balls in one hand and one in the other. Toss the front ball in the hand that has two. When it reaches its high point, throw the single ball in your other hand. When it reaches its high point, throw the remaining ball. Let them all drop!
6. Same as step 5, only this time catch the first toss.
7. Same as step 5, only this time catch the first two tosses. If you catch the first two balls and remember to throw the third, you will notice that there is only one ball remaining in the air, and you can already do one ball! We told you juggling was easy! Catch the third ball and you will experience your first juggulation. Celebrate!

Of course, now that you have experienced your first juggulation, you will no doubt wish to experience multiple juggulations. As you apply the Juggling Metaphor Method, focusing on the ease and direction of your throw and consciously letting the balls drop, you will enter the ecstatic realm of multiple juggulation. In the process you will learn how to improve the speed and quality of all your learning.

Index

MICHAEL J. GELB

Michael Gelb is a globally acclaimed pioneer in the fields of mind/body fitness, creative thinking, and leadership development. He is the founder and president of High Performance Learning, an international management training and consulting firm based in Great Falls, Virginia. HPL's clients include Du Pont, Amoco, Bell Atlantic, National Public Radio, and Merck. Michael Gelb is the author of the bestselling Nightingale-Conant audiotape program—*Mind Mapping: How to Liberate Your Natural Genius*. Gelb is the originator of the Juggling Metaphor Method and the concept of synvergent thinking, introduced in his book *Thinking for a Change*. Gelb is also the author of *BodyLearning: An Introduction to the Alexander Technique* and *Present Yourself: Captivate Your Audience with Great Presentations*. An avid practitioner and teacher of the martial art of aikido, Gelb is conducting research for his next book, *Black Belt Business*. He lives with his wife and two dogs in Great Falls, Virginia.

TONY BUZAN

Tony Buzan is the world's foremost authority on the application of brain research to improving human performance. He is the creator of Mind Maps, the originator of the concept of mental literacy, and is the founder of the Brain Trust. His classic *Use Both Sides of Your Brain* has sold more than two million copies worldwide. Tony's most recent books include *The Mind Map Book: Radiant Thinking*, which was named book of the year by the BBC, and *Buzan's Book of Genius*, to be released in the autumn of 1994. Buzan is a prize-winning poet and the author of nine other books on learning, memory and practical applications of brain research. His BBC television series *Use Your Head* is one of the most popular educational programs in the history of British television. Buzan's corporate clients include Digital Equipment Corp., Goldman Sachs, IBM, E.D.S., and many others. He is an official adviser to the British Olympic rowing and chess teams, a primary organizer of the World Memory Championships, and the International Mind Sports Olympiad. An accomplished rower, Buzan lives and works beside the river Thames near Henley, England.

Michael Gelb and Tony Buzan offer many programs on the themes expressed in this and their other books, including *The Mind and Body Seminar*, an extraordinary five-day residential program for leaders. For information on *The Mind and Body Seminar* and lectures, workshops, seminars, and consulting services offered by Michael Gelb and Tony Buzan, contact The High Performance Learning Center or The Buzan Centres (see over).

About The High Performance Learning Center® (HPL):
HPL is an international leadership training and consulting firm founded by Michael J. Gelb in 1982. It helps individuals and organizations define and realize their highest aspirations. HPL helps leaders "walk their talk" to build teamwork, creativity, communication, trust, and organizational alignment. A catalyst for cre-

ative change, HPL bridges the gap between visions of exceptional quality, superior service, personal fulfillment, and everyday behavior. HPL's most popular programs and services (customized to achieve specific client goals) include:

Mind Mapping and Creative Thinking
Presentation as Leadership
High Performance Sales
Black Belt Business®
Leadership, Vision, and Values
Lessons From the Art of Juggling
One-on-One Executive Coaching with Michael J. Gelb

Visual Synthesis®: Simultaneous, artistic illustration of the content of meetings, conferences, and strategic planning sessions by Nusa Maal Gelb

Contact:
Cathy Lewis, Director, Client Services
High Performance Learning®
9844 Beach Mill Road
Great Falls, Virginia 22066, USA
Telephone: (1) 703 757-7007
Fax: (1) 703 757-7211

Mind Mapping: How to Liberate Your Natural Genius by Michael Gelb is available in four audio-cassettes from Nightingale-Conant (2 Aspen Units, Aspen Way, Yalberton Industrial Estate, Paignton, Devon TQ4 7QR. Telephone: (44) 01803 666100. Fax: (44) 01803 557148).

About The Buzan Centres:
Buzan Centres were founded by Tony Buzan and Vanda North to teach the skills of Learning to Learn. Their focus is to apply the latest research on the brain to memory, learning, change, information management, reading, empowerment, quality, and life.

Courses from the Buzan Centres include the customized application of:
Radiant Thinking (Mind Maps®)
Radiant Remembering
Radiant Reading
Radiant Speaking
Radiant Selling
Each of these is a one-day course that may stand alone or be integrated with any existing training to increase its effectiveness. Public courses, in-company courses, or licensed train-the-trainer courses are also available.

Products from the Buzan Centres include the million-plus seller *Use Your Head* and the new *Mind Map Book*. Audiotapes include the new "Buzan On . . ." series, and other products include the new Charthouse video production, "If at first . . .," as well as Buzan Centres' Mind Map software and Life Management Systems. For more information on training, courses or products, contact Buzan Centres Ltd., 37 Waterloo Road, Bournemouth BH9 1BD, UK. Telephone: (44) 01202 533593. Fax: (44) 01202 534572.